Other publications by Ira Israel:

How To Survive Your Childhood Now That You're An Adult
A Path to Authenticity and Awakening

2017

Available through Amazon in paperback, e-book, and audio-book.

Ira Israel

WIRED & TIRED

A Guide to Revitalize Your Life

The contents of this book are intended for education and not intended to take the place of diagnosis and treatment by a qualified therapist or medical practitioner. If such level of assistance is required, the services of a qualified, competent professional should be sought. No expressed or implied guarantee of the effects of the use of the recommendations herein can be given or liability taken.

ISBN: 9798361710034 (paperback)

Cover design by Jennifer Markson

www.IraIsrael.com

To all of my teachers and students…

Thanks for teaching me so much!

Table of Contents

Preface

In general, if you are an adult human being functioning in Western civilization circa 2023, it would not be rocket science to discern why you think what you think and feel what you feel. The preponderance of people I meet feel over-worked, over-stimulated, under-loved, and under-appreciated. There's a particular malaise wafting over our society... it's as if we have gone off-course, lost what is essential to the human experience, and instead end up frittering away our days in front of sundry glass screens.

In short, we are wired & tired.

It doesn't often devolve into a full-blown panic attack resulting in a visit to the emergency room, or a major depressive episode, which is characterized by two weeks of symptoms resembling catatonia - the inability to perform the most basic of human functions. Wired & tired is more akin to dysthymia - a low-grade inability to take pleasure in almost anything. I've heard it called "lifestyle fatigue." There's just way too much to do, way too much to see, way too much to listen to, way too much to read, too many Zoom discovery conversations, too many social media posts...

It's overwhelming.

We bury our heads in our phones likes ostriches in the sand.

Ironically (if you can call it that), inhabitants of Western civilization enjoy more safety, freedom and privileges than almost any other culture that has ever existed. And yet, there are twin epidemics of anxiety (wired) and depression (tired) plaguing our society and contributing to seemingly infinite afflictions including our horrifying opioid addiction problem as well as our relatively high suicide rate.

One problem that this book addresses is the fact that we were never given "User's Manuals" for our minds and I will argue that most of what is taught in our educational systems prepares us to work - to be "productive members of society." Our educational system does not teach us how to live healthy, balanced lives full of love and thriving authentic relationships.

So let me ask you...

Has adult reality got you down?

Do the pressures of being "successful" make you think crazy shit, like walking into traffic or jumping off a bridge or taking your whole prescription for Xanax at once?

Has being over-committed made you stressed-out?

Do you have too many daily responsibilities?

Does FOMO (fear of missing out) make you over-commit yourself, then feel like a failure for flaking because you're just too tired to attend another function?

Have failed relationships made you jaded and mistrustful?

Have you or could you be diagnosed with depression, anxiety, ADHD, OCD or an addiction to shopping, food, video games, alcohol, drugs, debt, sex, porn or something else?

Or maybe you have accomplished all of your goals - house, partner, kids, cool vacations - and you still feel unsatisfied, wired & tired?

Have you become disillusioned, disenchanted or disappointed with your life in general?

How many times per month do you think, "I didn't sign up for this!"

"I didn't sign up for...

...all of these commitments...

...all of these subscriptions...

...infinite email solicitations...

...infinite software updates...

...never-ending upgrades...

...perpetual optimization...

...relentless pointless meetings - i.e., "Zoom discovery conversations"

...relationships that suck the life out of me...

...a profound lack of free time...

...the inability to pursue my dreams...

...feeling wired & tired all of the time!

Could it be that the previous legacy illusions and enchantments such as "the American Dream" - marriage for life and home-borrower-ship - no longer bring us the joy, satisfaction, contentment and happiness that they brought our parents and grandparents? Maybe you even feel enslaved to long-term commitments and contracts that are extremely difficult to quit?

How much of your autonomy did you surrender to meet someone else's definition of "the good life?"

How much agency have you really had in being the author and designer of your life?

Being an adult in Western civilization today can be distressing: as I write this, we are at the tail end of our first but not last global pandemic, there are myriad highly-volatile political situations nationally and internationally, a possible nuclear war, the majority of fellow humans face economic and/or food insecurity on a daily basis, and climate events - hurricanes, tornadoes, fires, earthquakes - perpetually wreak havoc on many people's lives with no end in sight. There's also a political sea change occurring that many people believe will culminate in sundry civil wars if not some sort of constant violent civil unrest or upheaval. Irrespective of personal political beliefs, most people would agree that our political system has been corrupted, does not work the way it was designed to work, and/or is now rigged or at least extremely unfair.

Raise your hand if you enjoy paying taxes, please.

Raise your hand again if you believe that your tax dollars are well-spent by the government.

Raise your hand if you think that the government has your best interests in mind when our representatives make new policies?

Do you feel that quotidian reality for most fellow Westerners has become more or less precarious and uncertain in the past 50 years?

As a thought experiment, please compare yourself to people who lived on the same soil one hundred years ago: millions of young men were conscripted to fight wars in Europe; millions of mothers and wives waited for weeks or months for mail from their sons and husbands. Many of them received dreaded knocks on their front doors from fellow soldiers and chaplains informing them that their loved one had been killed in battle.

Or how about 150-300 hundred years ago: immigrating by boat across the Atlantic, staking out some land to farm or going to work in a factory...

Or five hundred years ago: living in Europe under an aristoc-
racy and submitting to the whims of a king or queen...

On the one hand, most of us get quite unraveled at the
thought of going a few hours without running water and sewage
systems, or life without the electricity that powers our mobile
phones, computers and lights. And yet both toilets and electricity are relatively recent inventions. The first commercial cars and
airplanes were only born last century. How old is recorded sound
(egad - just imagine no background 80s music playing for us nos-
talgic Gen-Xers at Whole Foods!) or the first photograph? And
yet you would laugh at me if I asked to send you a fax (a black
and white facsimile of a piece of paper transmitted electronically
via zero and ones after being scanned by light and then sent
through a telephone line). Amidst all of these technological luxuries as well as all of the incredible advances science has made,
why are so many adults wired & tired?

I have organized this book in a manner that will help you
most expediently: the introduction is a brief deconstruction of
the Western paradigm, just to help you understand that there are
other perspectives, other possibilities - that it doesn't have to be
this way permanently. Then Part 1 provides both immediate solutions to being wired & tired and long-term practices and lifestyle choices that will help you revitalize your life. Being wired
& tired means that you are impatient and cannot wait until the
end of a book to get readily applicable tools and practices to alleviate your anxiety and depression - thus, I front-loaded this book
with solutions. Part 2 of the book (chapters 2 through 9) will
walk you through the sundry expected stages of life for adults in

our society and the usual corresponding crises and ruptures. As someone who has traversed his 20s, 30s, 40s, and most of my 50s, I will provide you with a 40,000-foot view of why adults think the things that we think during the various epochs of our adult lives and how we can think alternatively about those stages. Part 3 of this book will give a broad overview of subjects that you may have missed at university but would have helped you transcend the crises discussed in chapters 2 through 9, had you studied them. You will quickly note that I am an aggregator, meaning that I have covered a relatively wide breadth of the humanities over the past forty years of studying and I will offer you a few of the highlights with the intent of piquing your interest and inspiring you to go down rabbit holes of your own. I hope that the third part of this book provides an intellectual buffet that rejuvenates former passions, stimulates your mind, and inspires you to revitalize your life. Also, Part 3 will give you a new perspective on the sea change that Western civilization is currently going through, how we can be best prepared for it, and help engender a peaceful transition to the next society, if humanity as a species is able to avoid hemorrhaging itself off of the planet. It is incumbent upon all of us to "awaken" ASAP.

Some of the subjects in Part 3 may not seem interesting to you but I would argue that you learn more about a fellow human being by strolling around a museum discussing paintings, then you would by sitting at Starbucks interviewing them about their lives. Again, what is taught in our educational system prepares us how to work, not how to be in healthy, loving, compassionate, supportive relationships. There is no class in our school system that provides a "User's Manual" for our minds. This book is designed to help you think better, more propitiously. It will give you concise explanations and applicable solutions to typical ruptures in people's paradigms as well as quotidian crises and provide all of the scientifically proven tools to keep you at the higher range of your happiness spectrums for the rest of your life.

I want to plant the seed of you asking, "Why do I want what I want? What would need to occur for me to be truly content? How did I learn to desire what I desire? How do our desires differ from people from other cultures with different lifestyles? Can I make tweaks or adjustments to my own lifestyle that will engender more personal satisfaction?"

I hope to provoke the reader to gain new outlooks on various aspects of their lives at any age from 18 until 100 and thereafter. I remain adamant in my belief that our paradigms (the ways in which we see the world) are set at a very early age and some of our subconscious beliefs are even established before we learn to say "dada." Similarly, there are no definitive understandings regarding the malaise that is particular to human beings. My wish is that this book lends some comforting narratives regarding why we think what we think and how we can make healthier conscious decisions that will help us think in the most interesting, most compassionate, most loving, and most joyous ways possible.

PART 1

Introduction

"I don't know who discovered water but I doubt it was a fish." ~ Marshall McLuhan

What are the subconscious ramifications and most common psychological patterns that emerge from being raised in Western civilization, going to elementary and high school, and becoming prepared for college or university or to enter the workforce? What are unwitting problems caused by everything we consider to be "normal," i.e., capitalism, democracy, the myth of romantic love, etc.? In short, what are the common subconscious ramifications of growing up in America?

One theme I see emerging from our primary education system is that many people graduate from it believing that they think too much, that they can't get out of their heads, that they may have ADHD and/or anxiety. No baby was ever born thinking "too much" and no baby was ever born thinking "I'm not good enough." These are learned traits and I would argue that it is the highly competitive nature of our school system that is not setting its students up for calm, even-keeled, simple lives. The students are over-stimulated, they have way too many obligations, and there is pressure on them to study a bunch of shit that is totally uninteresting to them and seemingly inapplicable to their lives. Our educational system was designed to make laborers and over the last 200 years has transmuted into making crazy-people. Our educational system is traumatizing - even to the prom queen, even to the quarterback, even to the valedictorian…

the system does not facilitate the greatness of the majority of students; it leaves them feeling wired & tired.

Just for another perspective, in Atom Egoyan's film "Exotica," one of the main characters who has experienced terrible traumas says, "Nobody asks to be born." I suspect that many people who had the mandatory Western educational system inflicted upon them would agree with that phrase. And yet, billions of people - mostly from other cultures - might not agree. EDUCATION IS A PRIVILEGE and millions of people died fighting in wars so that you could be bullied by a group of mean girls in high school.

One thing we could agree on, though, is that these bodily incarnations of ourselves were previously non-existent for billions of years. They exist for a certain period of time and most of them age - grow bigger, then decline - in similar fashions and ultimately perish never to be seen again in the same bodily incarnations. Although there have been and are people attempting to freeze their bodies and physically reincarnate, the people who would disagree with the phrase "Nobody asks to be born" most likely believe in a soul or some form of ethereal consciousness that transmigrates from one incarnation to the next. We will explore these possibilities later in the discussions on spirituality, but for now just please understand that birth, as we understand it from our scientific Western paradigm, is simply what happens approximately nine months after a sperm fertilizes an egg. And from our perspective, YOU did not "ask" to be born anymore than you asked to be tortured in high school.

However, if your parents used the old-fashioned method of conceiving another albeit minuscule human being, approximately 100 million of your father's sperm cells rushed towards your mother's singular ovum in an attempt to fertilize it. One succeeded and the other approximately 99,999,999 died. So in one sense, even if you didn't "choose" to be born, your existence can easily be viewed as miraculous, as winning the lottery. The fact that that one sperm cell fertilized that one ovum - against all odds - to create YOU is astounding. So in one sense, your mere existence is akin to winning the lottery or as unlikely as being struck by lightning while being bitten by a shark.

But then you are "thrown," as Heidegger stated, into a world, the world, our world. Or what is often referred to as "reality" - with walls and ceilings and flashing lights and beds and couches and utensils and underwear and language and all sorts of clothing and accoutrements. As a baby you were 100% dependent on care-givers for your survival. Some animals are born and can walk on their own two or four feet and find food in minutes. Human beings need to be fed, cleaned, and protected for years or else they perish.

There are many individuation processes that enable the child to become fully independent. The first individuation process is when the baby becomes mobile (can escape predators by itself), is able to locate food, and learns to clean itself. In our culture, I suggest that toilet training would be a relative marker for this phase. However, during this time of weaning, I believe, along with many other Attachment Theorists, that there are subconscious patterns and or paradigms established. Babies want to eat when they are hungry, sleep when they are tired, defecate when they need to defecate and play when they feel playful. In order to help them become independent "productive" members of society, caregivers must DENY the baby from doing whatever it desires to do when it feels like doing it. Infants are put on feeding schedules, sleeping schedules, given play times, and ultimately when they go to school are given "bathroom breaks."

All of the above DENIAL of natural, present desires is what is considered to be "normal" in our society. What most people do not take into consideration is how terrifying these denials might be for the child as the caregivers train the infant to eat at mealtimes, play during play times, defecate during bathroom breaks and sleep through the night. Attachment Theory establishes relationship patterns that can emerge from how babies learn to individuate and take care of themselves. However, I also believe that there is deeper subconscious ingraining established in the infant's mind on whether the world is an inherently safe or dangerous place, and whether or not he or she can rely on, trust other people, and "securely attach." My extrapolating becomes wildly important when these infants become adults and engage in relationships with other humans. The 67% of people who "insecurely" attach to their primary caregivers as infants according to Mary Ainsworth, may have to strengthen certain emotional muscles as adults in order to transcend these insecurities and authentically attune and connect to other people.

This glossing over Attachment Theory - how we connect and relate to others during our entire lives - will become extremely important in the chapters regarding adult relationships and authentic happiness. For now it suffices to say that events occur - we may even call them "ruptures" - where children and adolescents must learn to stand on their own two feet. That their caregivers will not always be available to protect, feed, clean and amuse them. I would argue that the individuation processes can be traumatizing for some children and that some of their later adult fears or self-sabotaging could correlate to traumatic experiences that occurred twenty, thirty, forty years ago.

For a rather simplistic and common example (mostly witnessed in Soap Operas and French films), a partner may cheat on their spouse because during the individuation process they established the subconscious belief that other people will always abandon them; thus, they pre-emptively abandon their partner in order to stave off the reopening of their own primal abandonment wounds. Subconsciously this person will leave their computer open or phone unlocked in order for their spouse to catch their infidelity. Drama. Drama is like a Petri dish and people (mostly subconsciously) create it because they don't feel comfortable expressing their authentic fears; however, as we all know, drama has horrible unintentional consequences and can erode trust and damage security irreconcilably. This is why I teach authenticity, to preclude the subconscious creation of drama, to preclude people from burning down their own and their neighbors' emotional houses just to be able to utter a few sentences that they had previously been too scared to utter.

Again, the point is that whatever information you have about your infancy will help you firstly create a narrative of why you are who you are, why you think what you think, and why you desire what you desire; secondly, after you have that narrative you can decide whether it is most propitious for you to lean into various situations or flee them. Because at base, fight-flight-freeze remains a primal governing factor of our more extreme reactions. That mechanism is deeply ingrained in our hardware, so we should at least be aware of how, when, and why it gets triggered. In much of modern society, we are safe from predators so our fight-flight-freeze response is unnecessary. However, primal fears can be triggered (mostly by unexpected stimuli from intimate relationships) and our bodies can resort to these animal behaviors. From personal experience as well as witnessing couples in therapy for 16 years, I can tell you that it doesn't bode well when one partner in a relationship "shuts down" (freezes) because it usually signals abandonment to the other partner who then may be provoked to subconsciously fight or flee. Again, any fight-flight-freeze reactions are usually dramatic and could be precluded if we felt sufficiently safe to authentically express ourselves.

The first individuation process occurs when the infant is mobile and taking care of his or her own needs independently of the caregivers but for the most part caregivers are always in the vicinity. The second individuation process takes place when the infant (2-5 years old) is dropped off at school for the first time with new caregivers and other infants. For the sake of argument let's assume that being brought up in a highly competitive, capitalistic first-world country unintentionally accelerates the individuation process. However, let's entertain the possibility that the psychological ramifications could actually be much more dire than I am conveying: according to the founder of primal therapy, Arthur

Janov, when a baby is put down alone for the first time — say, in its own room while the parents sleep in another room — and allowed to "cry itself out" (cry until it is so exhausted that its only option is to fall asleep), the baby registers being "put down" as: "Why are you leaving me alone to die? You are killing me!" (Yes, I am intentionally making a pun: "put down" means "lay to sleep" with infants but "euthanize" with pets.) Janov argues that being put down for the first time creates a core, or primal, betrayal/abandonment wound in many people. Later in life, according to this theory, when our partner cheats on us or we are fired from a job we love, we become distraught because this betrayal/abandonment reopens our core betrayal/abandonment wound. Babies simply want to be loved and taken care of; when they feel abandoned, they sense their own dependence on others and their own lack of autonomy, and they tend to freak out.

So the unwitting ramifications of infants being "put down" to sleep alone and then "sent off" to school (until the child becomes acclimated to these new realities) is what I call, after Janov, a "primal betrayal/abandonment wound." As animals, I believe that we are supposed to be in our mother's arms and sleeping with our primary caregivers - provided a secure environment - for four or so years. But the highly competitive nature of late capitalism has caused people to shorten this secure stage when the baby's needs are taken care of in the name of creating "productive" members of society as early as possible. A **longer** earning potential is a **greater** earning potential. However, one of the themes of my previous book, "How To Survive Your Childhood Now That You're An Adult," is that our rather abrupt individuation processes have created a majority of INSECURE people whose abandonment fears (cf. the imposter syndrome) manifest as anxiety and depression or to what I am referring to as "wired & tired." One of the many reasons that so many Americans are currently being treated for anxiety and depression can be traced back to the traumas associated with an infant gaining its own sense of self, its own identity, and how resilient the baby is.

What is important in terms of personal identity is how these traumas are interpreted and assimilated. If an infant is securely attached to his or her mother and/or primary caregivers, then it subconsciously knows that the mother would never really put it in harm's way; from Mary Ainsworth's "Strange Situation" experiments in 1969 we know that infants with secure attachment (33% according to Ainsworth) do not freak out when the mother leaves them alone. The world is essentially safe to them. And more importantly, they can securely reattach when the mother returns. However, the Doctor Spock/Nietzschean — "let the baby cry itself out," "what doesn't kill it makes it stronger" — parenting style of previous generations may correlate with the spate of divorcees who do not truly know how to securely attach and reattach due to the stark and abrupt individuations that were forced upon them before they could speak. The world is essentially unsafe to them. Just as a thought experiment, imagine a family on a desert island and how they would interact for the first four years of their child's life and compare it to our bottle-fed, raised by a nanny from a foreign country, sleeps in its own cage and/or swaddled a few weeks after birth, etc. The "scientific" way of raising children seems to have starkly different mandates than a child being raised in nature.

No child was ever born with low self-esteem.

My proposal is that one result of our way of raising children in Western civilization is low self-esteem. Rampant low self-esteem. Children assimilate the frowns of their caregivers trying to train them to use a fork as "There must be something wrong with ME. Mommy (or whatever "Other" "mOther" in Lacanian terms) would not be unhappy if I were perfect." Thus, many infants assimilate the idea that "There must be something wrong with ME" during the first 0-4 years of their lives and this low self-esteem dogs them through adult years of addiction, infidelity, self-sabotage, inability to maintain a job, and many of the afflictions listed in the thousands of pages of cognitive and emotional disorders listed in the Diagnostic and Statistical Manual of Mental Disorders.

Additionally, our educational system is very cliquey: when children are making same-aged friends and forming cliques at school, they notice that they are EXCLUDED from some groups. Again, it is possible that these phenomena are assimilated as "There must be something wrong with ME. If I were different/cooler/perfect/taller/etc. then that group would accept me." The funny thing is that I would say that the majority of people (and I admit that my psychotherapy clients represent a skewed population) believe they are "outsiders." There is something perverse about our culture that makes most people — even the prom queen, football quarterback, movie star, rock star, tech billionaire — feel marginalized. This could be a result of the splintering of our society but until we find or create some common core values like compassion, then it will remain difficult for people from different "tribes" - geeks, jocks, yuppies, millennials, Bobos, Republicans, Democrats, Progressives, Socialists, to name a few - to communicate empathetically with each other.

Ah… what can be said about teenage years that hasn't already been documented on Netflix and HBO? It's all about angst, seemingly. Why are these years so arduous for the unwilling participants? Is it the hormonal changes? Peer pressure? The desire to be liked amidst a sea of haters. Continuously being judged, weighed, calculated, squeezed into a box? There's something so desperate about being a teenager in our culture. The resentment accrued during this phase of individuation is monstrous and manifests ultimately as low self-esteem.

Teenage suicide rates have never been higher. And "School Shootings" are a distinctly American phenomena. It appears as if there are severe growing pains associated with being a teenager in Western civilization. In recent times, thanks to technology and disease, things seem to have grown even worse. Most Gen Z-ers today equate texting and DM-ing with "talking" — lest we inform them that 93% of all communications are non-verbal, according to UCLA psychology professor Albert Mehrabian. But even when they see each other on FaceTime or Zoom it is usually only the face so that all body language and ethereal energy as well as smells and chemistry (pheromones) are completely missing.

Mirror neurons do not fire via text message.

As I will argue at the end of this book, future adults should be taught classes such as, "How to be someone's friend," "How to give a non-creepy hug," "How to actively listen and make other people feel heard," "How to have loving relationships," and "How to breathe lovingly" rather than forced to learn subjects that they will never use later in life. We need to figure out another way of interacting that is more compassionate so that future adults are able to construct secure attachments and stronger self-worth. Alas… this book is not for teenagers, not even disguised as Vikings at Burning Man. It is for adults whose greatness will be facilitated by transcending and overcoming any malaise developed during while growing up.

That is a brief overview of the psychological ramifications of growing up in Western civilization in the 21st century. Infancy, adolescence and teenage years are awkward and confusing for everyone involved: too many choices, too many influences, too much in-fighting, too much competition… in some ways our educational system could be equated to a giant resentment factory where spirits are crushed, souls are destroyed, and many teenagers emerge as faceless laborers duped in producing odd and often useless luxuries or manipulating symbols on glass screens for the next 60 years or until a sufficient rupture compels them to discard the measures of success that have become gilded cages and self-induced slavery.

Our entire educational system should be razed and rebuilt from the ground upward. Until that day, do not expect any decline in the teenage suicide rate nor in school shootings. The first eighteen years of a human's life should not be one behavior-modification exercise after another because one unintentional ramification of continuously being graded and judged is low self-esteem.

Chapter 1. Solutions

This chapter will provide scientifically proven tools to keep you at the high end of your happiness range for the rest of your life. *Authentic happiness.*

But first, allow me to summarize the numerous factors that added up to your current state of discontent.

The primary responsibility of our minds is to keep us safe, secure, and out of harm's way; it does this by taking the traumas of the past and projecting them into the future, simultaneously creating resentments: resentments are when you want something to be different that is impossible to change. I resented that I had scars on my face. Some people resent that their parents got divorced, that they were forced to go to schools they didn't want to go to, that their sibling was supposedly favored by their parents, that they were humiliated or violated or oppressed or molested in some way. If we live bound to our childhood resentments, our initial insecure attachment dynamics, our unforgiveness, our low self-esteem and all of our compensations for childhood traumas then we are signing up for a life of depression and anxiety. In short, your best shot at happiness is to show up authentically as an adult and jettison the false self you created to get your emotional and psychological needs met when you were growing up.

So in the grand scheme of reality, the crisis or rupture that you experienced that led you to this book crushed your faith in the reality into which you were thrown and didn't really question: the systems of our educational system, labor, capitalism, our form of democracy, working 40 hours in 5 days per week, fossil fuels, pharmaceuticals, vacations, status symbols - all of the things that most people consider to be "normal." But now you know that this "normal" does not bring with it happiness. Actually, this "normal" causes many people to be wired & tired. So you are reading this book because you want to minimize anxiety and depression, you want to construct a life that will be more favorable for keeping you at the higher range of your happiness spectrum. From a Harvard longitudinal study, we know that the primary thing that correlates with happiness is the quality of our intimate relationships. From the studies on Attachment Theory, we all know that most of us have fairly unrefined tools to being in intimate relationships. My proposal is that our best shot for being in secure relationships is to learn how to be authentic. To make conscious choices and to have the personal integrity to abide by those choices. To be congruent. To know why we think the shit that we think (and by 'shit' I mean our fears and prejudices, the paradigms we developed from our insecure attachment dynamics) and to lean into being vulnerable and authentic.

Firstly, here is a list of TOOLS to help when you are not just wired & tired but truly in fight-flight-freeze mode, when your mind is circling the drain, and you need immediate relief:

1. The three-part breath

Due to the fact that we are sitting most of the day and jacking up our energy levels with caffeine, protein and sugar, unbeknownst to us we are in almost continuous states of fight or flight mode, which is perpetuated by taking staccato breaths into just the bottom of our lungs. For this exercise we think of our lungs as having three parts: the lower third that we can feel expand and contract through the bottom of the front ribs; the middle third that we can feel expand and contract through the thoracic spine; and the upper third that we can feel expand and contract near the clavicle bone at the bottom of the neck. I like to say, "Inhale two three four; Exhale two three four" about 10 times as if I'm conducting a symphony. Inhaling, the "two" correlates to inhaling breath into the bottom of the lung, the "three" represents the middle of the lung, and the "four" represents the clavicle. Exhaling, the "two" correlates to the clavicle, the "three" correlates to the middle of the lung, and the "four" correlates to the bottom. We have the ability to take ourselves out of fight or flight mode by doing the three-part breath for 3-5 minutes. For people who suffer from anxiety or think they may be starting to have a panic attack I recommend this exercise.

2. Meditate

Meditation is a practice and is extremely challenging for goal-oriented people. If you were raised in a "not good-enough" society like ours, it will always feel like we should be meditating "better" or "more." Also, meditation often doesn't feel as if it is "working" or effective because you can usually only appreciate its effect retroactively. This is exactly where the learning exists: in being humbled by the simplest possible task - to sit. Just sit. And release expectations. Observe your mind as it barrages you with inane and maladaptive thoughts. It's actually quite humorous if you can observe the segues between thoughts. It may seem counter-intuitive to suggest such a potentially daunting and frustrating exercise to take us out of fight or flight mode, but the ability to shift our internal paradigms and direct our awareness towards more pleasant thoughts (i.e., gratefulness, gratitude) is a usually quite rewarding.

Here are some things to keep in mind while ameliorating being wired & tired through meditation:

1. Be an under-achiever. Just sit in the proper position with the spine straight, hips higher than the knees, chin level and face relaxed, and take ten deep inhalations and ten deep exhalations.

2. Invert science: instead of thinking of yourself as a pair of lungs ingesting air through your nose and esophagus, imagine that you are a drop of water in the ocean, that the universe is breathing THROUGH you rather than you are an individual human body sucking in breaths of air.

3. Revel in the paradoxes of life made analogous by the paradox of meditation: you are alert yet relaxed. Alert yet relaxed - just think about it for a second. For me, my bones and my frame are rigid and still; gravity gently guides my flesh into melting towards the earth.

4. Revel in the uncertainty. Human beings crave certainty and often entertain absurd possibilities about the future as contingency plans. The mind's primary job is to try to stave off potential future trauma. It does this by continuously recycling traumas from the past and projecting them into the future. However, the future is an amorphous void. Meditation harnesses the mind into the present so that it stops imaging possible future catastrophes. Learn to revel in the fact that the future is uncertain and that all you really have is the present moment, right here, right now.

5. Learn how to observe your thoughts like clouds passing through the sky rather than like wild horses dragging you around. YOU are not your thoughts. The brain is the hardware

and the mind is the software. If your mind is spinning out then you need to REBOOT THE HARD-DRIVE and clear the cache.

3. Yoga

The second yoga sutra of Patanjali is that "Yoga stills the fluctuations of the mind. Then the true self can appear." As I mentioned above, your essential "Self," whatever you consider that to be, is NOT your thoughts. Your thoughts merely trick you into thinking that they are the be-all and end-all but I'm sure you would bet that many of your family members have survived quite well without having any meaningful thoughts in years. If you're wired & tired then your mind is probably "un-still." It's probably fluctuating fairly rapidly. Yoga was designed to still the fluctuations of the mind. I've been known to tell my yoga students, "If I hadn't discovered yoga thirty years ago, I'd probably be dead or in jail." If you're spinning out, take a yoga class ASAP.

4. Cardio - run, swim, bike, etc.

There's this thing called science and science has informed us that endorphins are released in the brain when you elevate your heart rate for thirty minutes or more. If you're feeling wired & tired and you need to immediately de-stress yourself then please enjoy thirty minutes of your favorite cardiovascular exercise as soon as possible.

5. Nature

Walks in nature are usually quite calming. I enjoy walks along the beach because the Pacific Ocean makes me feel extremely small. There's an entire universe outside of my mind and viewing it, smelling it and feeling different types of breezes caress my face is often sufficient to recalibrate my nervous system.

6. Replace the resentments that your mind creates with gratitude

Rick Hanson taught me, "You can't pull all of the weeds in the garden. But you can plant flowers." Our minds were designed to create woulda-coulda-shoulda-didn't resentments - to want things to be more/different/better - and these resentments are the root cause of our suffering. We cannot remove the resentments but we can displace them. We do this by planting flowers of gratitude. This is what is known in Cognitive Behavioral Therapy as gratitude lists. I recommend setting the bar as low as possible.

For instance:
I am grateful that...
1. I have 2 legs
2. I have human consciousness
3. I have a few loving friends
4. I have a roof over my head
5. I have enough money to eat today

There are millions and millions - nay, billions - of fellow human beings who are not as fortunate as many of us are. Appreciation for the privilege and freedoms that you and I enjoy often can lift us out of the malaise that accompanies being wired & tired. Gratitude lists are simple and effective ways to raise consciousness immediately. Trust me, the situation could always be worse. And writing a few positive aspects about our current situations is usually quite uplifting.

7. Reframing

Looking at what we consider to be problems through alternative lenses usually provides a little relief. Think of a problem:

When and where do you have this problem?

Who are you when you have this problem?

What are you aiming to achieve when you have this problem?

What do you believe about yourself when you have this problem

What skills do you have that enable you to have this problem?

How could you teach someone else how to have your problem?

How could you teach someone else to not have the problem?

What skills would you need to STOP having this problem?

Reframing enables you to see what you are considering to be a "problem" through other lenses. Just to be provocative, I will recount an adage I heard some time ago: "Any problem that can be solved by money isn't a problem." There are often alternative ways to think about the things that we consider to be problems and are stressing us out.

8. Alternate nostril breath to balance masculine/feminine energies

Nadi Shodhana. There are countless nadi shodhana demonstration videos on YouTube. I like to hold up the right hand then fold down the first two fingers so that we can use the thumb to block off the right nostril and the ring finger and pinky to block off the left nostril. Like the three-part breath, I like to block off the right nostril then take a long fluid breath into the left nostril. You can count off 4 or 6 or 8 seconds, whichever feels good for you; then we block off the left nostril and exhale through the right nostril for the same 4, 6 or 8 seconds. Then we inhale through the left and exhale through the right for the same durations. There are many ways to practice nadi shodhana but if you believe Indian sages as well as Carl Jung, the right side of your body contains male energy while the left side contains female energy. Nadi shodhana balances your male and female energies.

9. "What can we do to facilitate each other's greatness?"

Eckhart Tolle says in "The Power of Now" that the only reason you should be in a relationship is because you want to learn. I actually think that couples should work to facilitate each other's greatness. As a "Pattern Interrupt," in order to discombobulate the other person's defensiveness, I like to have one of the partners ask, "What can I do to facilitate your greatness? I can't be great unless you're great. What can I do to facilitate that?" Try saying that to someone in your family and see what type of reaction you receive.

10. Visit a museum

Having spent all of my adult life in major cities, I have enjoyed quietly strolling through art museums and wondering about the artists who created the paintings and sculptures and what they were trying to express. In particular I am a great fan of Barnett Newman, Ellsworth Kelly, and Mark Rothko's paintings so if I need to recalibrate my nervous system, I have found that an hour or two standing or sitting in front of particular colors, shapes, and stories really helps my spirit and feeds my soul.

Bonus: Try one of Paul McKenna's Hypnotic Inductions

Paul McKenna has graciously made many of his hypnotic inductions available on YouTube. If your mind is circling the drain, then let Mister McKenna help you reprogram it.

And now here are 10 long-term daily practices to add to your life to help preclude being wired & tired:

1. Know how you self-sabotage and how to auto-correct

If we recognize patterns that are hindering authentic relationships, that constitutes self-sabotage. Or we show up late for work or miss meetings - that is also self-sabotage. We have to recognize when we are not showing up with personal integrity to meet our commitments and see that as self-sabotage and cease such behavior immediately.

Personally I love Fred Luskin's problem-solving exercise to help people understand how we are hard-wired maladaptively.

Please take a pen and a piece of paper and write down any problem or several problems in your life.

For example:

PROBLEM(S): the brakes on my car didn't last 60,000 miles and now I have to spend time and money unexpectedly getting them replaced. Or... my kids don't return my text messages. Or... my boss doesn't give me enough vacation time. Write down any problem or problems in your life.

Then write down any THOUGHTS you have about that problem or those problems.

For example:

THOUGHTS: The brakes should have lasted 60,000 miles. My kids should return my text messages in a timely fashion. My boss should give me more vacation time. My 401k should not have gone down.

Then write down any EMOTIONS you feel about the problem:

For example:

FEELINGS: I feel frustrated, I feel ripped-off, I feel disappointed, I feel sad, I feel as if my work isn't respected, I feel betrayed, I feel abandoned...

Then write down any ACTIONS that revolve around or result from that problem.

For example:

ACTIONS: I find myself shopping online for new cars in the middle of the night. I find myself shopping online for lawyers who will take on a class-action lawsuit against the automobile company that promised my brakes would last 60,000 miles. I find myself passive-aggressively not responding to my kids' text messages to make them understand how disrespectful they are. I binge eat. I binge drink. I binge shop. I binge xxxxxx. I blocked the fucker. I show up late for meetings.

You now have a piece of paper that looks like this:

PROBLEM:

THOUGHTS:

FEELINGS:

ACTIONS:

Next please circle all of the THOUGHTS, FEELINGS and ACTIONS that SOLVE the original problem.

Usually when we do this exercise there is silence, then nervous laughter ensues. After about 30 seconds I say, "That's right, your thoughts, feelings and actions DON'T solve your problems. Most of us are hard-wired for failure. We are hard-wired maladaptively. If you look closely, you'll probably realize that your THOUGHTS, FEELINGS and ACTIONS actually MAKE YOUR PROBLEMS WORSE!"

Thus, we can all recognize that what we consider to be "normal" and "rational" cognition for many of us perpetuates a state of being wired & tired. There are incessant chores and tasks to "do." Much of the time the list of things on our "to-do" list is daunting and overwhelming. We need to be able to detach, unplug, and relax.

2. Work a daily meditation practice into your schedule

My favorite meditations are visualizations where we put our thoughts as they exist in the form of sentences such as "I have to put the laundry in the dryer after meditation" onto either a leaf floating down a stream, a cloud floating through the sky, or a cartoon thought-bubble floating to the top of a pool and watch that thought float away. We do this repeatedly and once we get the hang of it; we can feel the distance between the watcher and the thoughts. The fact is - even if you're an atheist - that YOU are not (just) thoughts. Although your thoughts often trick you into thinking that they're the most important things in the world - all-encompassing, and crucial - you can learn how to dis-identify with them and give your mind a much-needed rest. You cannot tell the mind what NOT to think and the mind does not have an "off" switch. But you can learn how to observe your thoughts, watch them pass through your mental mindscreen, and actively CHOOSE not to react to them. Later in the day, long after this meditation wherein you have CULTIVATED NON-REACTIVITY, you can choose to let things that used to trigger you pass through you rather than stir up a reaction. As seen in the Fred Luskin exercise, many of our instantaneous reactions are maladaptive. Thus, learning how to cultivate non-reactivity by observing our thoughts will help us make healthier long-term decisions in all circumstances.

My next favorite meditation is the Metta Meditation, which helps to create a microcosm of safety, health and well-being - albeit temporarily.

For Metta meditations we usually practice them by reciting something such as:

May I be safe.

May I be happy.

May I be healthy.

May I live with ease.

Then we can wish the same things for a loved one, a stranger, someone with whom we have difficulties, and then for ourselves again. "Loving-kindness" (Metta) is always available to us, and this meditation creates a loving container and makes us aware of how much fear and needless animosity we consider to be "normal" in our lives. After going through the meditation for other beings we usually conclude by wishing safe, happiness, health and ease for all sentient beings:

May all beings be safe.

May all beings be happy.

May all beings be healthy.

May all beings live with ease.

Lastly, after practicing yoga or meditation I sit and put my hands in prayer pose at my heart then raise my thumbs to my forehead and ask for "Clarity of consciousness (for the rest of this beautiful day"); then I lower my thumbs to my lips and ask for "Clarity of communications (with all of my friends and loved ones and with whomever I come into contact with - for the rest of this beautiful day"); then I lower my thumbs back to my heart and ask for "Clarity of sentiment (for the rest of this beautiful day"). When this exercise is practiced in the morning it usually establishes a steady anchor for even-keel regulation for the rest of the day.

To summarize, I'm a huge advocate of creating a morning ritual that starts the day off most propitiously. For that includes making a smoothy, doing some sun salutations while my cat scampers in the grass outside, meditating and then setting the intention for the day - namely, clarity of consciousness, communications, and sentiment.

3. "Clap last Thursday"

Eckhart Tolle says, "Either accept your life or change it; any other position is insane." We cannot change the past, which is why when I teach, I ask students to raise their hands and on the count of three to "Clap last Thursday." Obviously, this is a pattern-interrupt. The students are flummoxed because you cannot clap last Thursday and this is instantly proven to them somatically and viscerally that they cannot go back in time. Thus, the sooner we accept the past and OWN how we got to today, the sooner we ameliorate our own suffering. We cannot change the past, what good does it do to complain about it? Anytime our mind says, "I would be happy now if,... x happened or y didn't happen" we are creating your own suffering. The phrase "Clap last Thursday" serves as a gentle reminder to change the things we can and accept the things we cannot change.

4. Marshall Rosenberg's Non-violent communications in order to reduce blame

I inspire people to be vulnerable, own their own emotional experiences, and reduce blaming others by employing one of Marshall Rosenberg's Non-violent Communications exercises:

I feel _____
(a feeling state)

when _____
(something you observe happens)

because I need _____.
(an emotional need)

In the future, could you please_____.
(a request)

You cannot tell someone to be vulnerable but you can IN-SPIRE them by MODELING it for them. Non-violent communications is a wonderful tool to help you inspire loved ones show up in a non-blamey manner.

5. "How do we make this a win-win situation?"

Herbert Spencer's dictum "Survival of the fittest" meant that life was a zero-sum game with winners and losers. This belief regarding supposed inherent competitiveness destroys relationships and is destroying the planet. Harville Hendrix once said, "You can either be right or you can be in relationship." Instead of having a situation with a winner and loser, the parties should ask each other "How can we make this a win-win situation?" Honestly, whenever there is any sort of conflict or disagreement in a relationship, I ask partners to turn to each other and ask, "How can we make this a win-win situation?" And if they cannot figure out how to make it a win-win situation at present, I ask them to at least "agree to disagree."

6. Love Languages: Quality time, Words of Affirmation, Gifts, Acts of Service, Physical Touch

If you're in an intimate relationship, it behooves you to tell your partner what your love languages are and to ask what they're love languages are. I've seen couples where one person will buy the other a $4,000 present but the person's love language is Words of Affirmation, thus the present is meaningless. Couples need to know what they like to receive - what registers to them as "love" and what they enjoy giving as a symbol of love. Then they need to be on the same page so that they can stop claiming to have given symbols of love that completely missed the mark.

7. Cleaning up the past in order to show up authentically for the present moment

Forgiveness and self-forgiveness. This realizing of "Atonement" is sometimes a process so adding some forgiveness and self-forgiveness into your meditation or adding some time to journal and reflect up whatever does not serve you - anger, resentments, etc. - and release them, usually helps to lighten our daily loads.

8. Accident Victims and Lottery Winners

A scientific study regarding happiness was conducted that showed that human beings underestimate their resilience and overestimate the things that would make us happy. Most people would say things like, "If I won $100 million dollars in the lottery I'd never complain again!" But that's not accurate. In about 18 months whatever level of happiness you were at before you won the lottery you want to fall back into. Similarly, if you were in an awful car accident and suffered from broken bones etc., after about 18 months you would be back to whatever level of happiness you were at before the car accident. This is why Positive Psychologists call it a "Happiness Spectrum" - because as long as we engage in constant healthy practices that keep us at the higher end of that spectrum, extreme events will not disable us dramatically. Remind yourself that your mind overestimates things that would make you happy; this will probably help you avoid impulse purchases because the dopamine hit you receive from a frenzied impulsive shopping victory will dissipate sooner than you imagine.

9. Agency: Be More Proactive

Many people feel as if they have attained certain measures of success and can take it easier thereafter. Human beings crave NOVELTY and novelty doesn't usually come knocking on a closed door. At 40 years old I started riding a motorcycle, at 50 I started taking French classes at UCLA, at 52 I took boxing classes for the first time, at 53 I took up tennis for the first time since high school, at 54 I started swimming classes. Being proactive - trying new things - is what keeps us vibrant. If you want to be authentically happy then I advise being proactive in exploring new activities and interests.

10. Learn how to optimize fueling your body

It is best to assume that everything that we learned about food growing up is wrong. Most of us eat for psychological reasons more than to fuel our bodies. I'm not a nutritionist but we all need to learn what fuel is needed to optimize our physical bodies as well as our thoughts and emotions. Try different combinations, different serving sizes, different times and figure out what is best for your body and mind to run as smoothly as possible.

Bonus: Congruence - deciding the life you want to create

Congruence entails mitigating hypocrisy. It is having who we are match who we know we should be. It sounds simple but it is essential to authentic happiness. Make a commitment to personal integrity. Write down who you know you should be, what personal characteristics you should embrace, and then figure out a how you are going to live congruently and with no regrets!

OK, so as I state - or rather dare - students in my live courses, you are either going to leave this book with new solutions and results, or with excuses. Change is difficult - we fear change - and I hope that my passion for psychology, philosophy, spirituality and other subjects is infectious; I hope that it inspires you to try new solutions to old problems.

To summarize, here is a list of some of the tools that I believe will bring you both immediate and long-term changes and results:

- The 3-part breath to take you out of fight or flight mode
- The problem-solving exercise to remember that we're often our own worst enemies
- Clap last Thursday: you can't change the past
- Metta Meditation - be the change you want to see in the world
- Clarity of consciousness, communication and sentiment
- Replace the resentments your mind creates with gratitude - write gratitude lists
- Reflective listening to help make others feel heard

- Non-violent communications to express yourself authentically without blame
- Nadi Shodhana to balance your energies
- Forgiveness to clean up your resentments
- Accident Victims, Lottery Winners - things you think will make you happy will definitely make you happy but not for as long as you think they will
- Yoga to still the fluctuations of the mind
- Mindfulness meditations - learn to observe your thoughts rather than allowing them to drag you around
- Congruence - deciding the life you want to lead and then figuring out how to create that life

And here are some of the excuses I've heard in my classes when people are unwilling to try new solutions:

- I didn't care for Ira
- I was overwhelmed by the material
- I've heard it all before
- I don't agree with Ira's politics
- This stuff is way too bohemian for me
- Way too religious for me
- Too woo-woo for me
- Is "Ira Israel" a stage name?
- I have a migraine
- I think I missed some of the essential parts in the beginning
- Doesn't Ira know long hair is out of style?
- I'm too tired to read!
- I can't concentrate!
- (enter a new excuse you might use here)
- (enter your usual excuse here)

Again, please allow me to summarize one of my main theses: the only thing that correlates strongly with authentic happiness - not being wired & tired - is the quality, the connection, the security and dependability of our intimate relationships. If we want to have secure intimate relationships then we need to be authentic. Unfortunately we live in a culture where we were taught to create shiny inauthentic one-dimensional facades. Usually ruptures in our paradigm cause us to go into crisis and re-evaluate our measures of success as well as what makes us truly happy - that's what Part 2 of this book is about, the ruptures. And when the ruptures occur they often provoke us to incorporate new sets of tools and practices that are propitious for keeping us at the high end of our happiness spectrums. "If you always do what you always did then you'll always get what you've always gotten," is a popular adage. I hope that the above lists of immediate solutions and long-term practices provide a road map for you to try some new paths when the ruptures delineated in Part 2 occur.

PART 2

Typical Adult Crises by age group

Part 2 of this book discusses the typical crises that adults experience in our culture. My intention here is to lend solace to anyone in crisis by making them feel that 1. they are not alone and 2. it's not (all) their fault. In general, I hope to demonstrate that most of the things we consider to be problems are situational, cultural, and would not exist if we grew up in a tribe on a desert island and lived in huts with our extended families and had ample supplies of fresh fruit and seafood. All of us were "thrown" into a particular society at a particular time and although there are remarkable privileges to living in Western civilization in the 2020s - relatively robust health and longer life spans - there are many pressures and stresses and influences causing many of us to feel wired & tired.

Chapters 2 & 3 will discuss jobs and relationships for people 20 to 30 years old; chapters 4 and 5 will discuss careers and families for people approximately 30-45 years-old; chapter 6 is literally a joke, chapter 7 relates to people usually around 45-65 who are experiencing existential mid-life crises for the first time, chapter 8 provides my philosophy regarding happiness and chapter 9 deals with retirement.

If you have ever watched anyone do a "cold reading" as part of a mentalism performance or magic show, you will understand that I'm not employing any psychic abilities in Part 2. In some general manner, whether we've become addicted to drugs or sports or are getting divorced or hate our jobs, we are all clichés in some way - we are all "stereotypical" - with the rare exceptions of true outliers, rogues and icon-oclasts and even those people are constrained by language and media. Thus, it is not rocket-science to discern or guess - in general - why you think the things that you think. And although many of us feel margin-alized - like outsiders, pariahs - the fact of the matter is that many of our thoughts are somewhat predictable, which is why magic and com-edy are so much fun: because our minds are so easily fooled.

Chapter 2. First Jobs, 20-30 years-old

If you read "How To Survive Your Childhood Now That You're An Adult," you will recall that I state that parenting is the most difficult job in the world. It's difficult because parents are trying to instill mutually exclusive psychological attributes in their children: parents are trying to instill healthy self-esteem and healthy self-regulation. If parents are too oppressive and emotionally withholding, children will grow up with great self-regulation but low self-esteem; if parents are too admiring and laissez-faire then children will grow up with high self-esteem but low self-regulation. Although we consider people 18 years-old and older to be adults in our society - we consider them sufficiently reasonable to vote but not to drink alcohol - these chapters deals with the final individuation process, when younger adults graduate college, and in my generation lived alone for the first time, got full-time jobs and paid for our own rent, food, and possibly even health insurance and accouterments for the first time. Currently younger adults can remain on their parent's health insurance policies until they are 26 so the real indicator of a true adult in our society appears to be if they pay their own mobile phone bill or remain on some parent's or someone's family plan.

I imagine that if you attended and graduated from university that you spent the second part of your senior year partying and possibly looking for your first full-time job with health insurance, benefits, maybe stock options. Let us assume that you found your first full-time job after graduating and now are trying to live a balanced life. Unless you are working for a close relative, leading a balanced life is going to be damn near impossible. Our labor system is based on oppression and exploitation so at some point during your first or second year of indentured servitude after college, working 80-100 hours per week, it will appear reasonable to you to blow your brains out. You might get by anesthetizing yourself with drugs, alcohol, video games, and shopping for some time, but you will soon learn that our form of highly competitive capitalism includes its own form of hazing and that the lowest person on the totem pole will be expected to work and produce and labor until their soul and spirit has been ripped out of their bodies, crushed on the floor in front of their eyes, and danced upon by their bosses and peers. In short, it is going to be almost impossible for anyone working their first job NOT to feel wired & tired.

College will seem like four years of Club Med by the time you finish your first year working.

But if that seems bad please know that it's 1,000 times worse than I just described. Mostly due to the fact that nobody taught you how to have healthy relationships with money, food, alcohol, video games, sex, drugs, etc. Unless you are some sort of freak exception, your autonomy has been foreclosed and unbeknownst to you, you have become an indentured servant, basically a slave. A hefty paycheck might help you delude yourself that this couldn't possibly be enslavement, but the money is just like putting lipstick on a pig.

Prozac, Paxil, Wellbutrin, Lexapro, Klonopin, Cymbalta anyone?

Human beings crave autonomy and agency.

Autonomy is our ability to decide what we are going to do and when we are going to do it.

Agency is our ability to execute those decisions.

After meeting thousands of clients and students, I have concluded that autonomy and agency correlate inversely with our society's twin epidemics of anxiety and depression - wired & tired. And since our labor system believes that the young workers have to "pay their dues," we squeeze every morsel of labor possible out of them; hence, I have worked with a plethora of 22-30 year- old adults who have little autonomy or agency; if you look closely, as young adults spend a few years at one company, they realize that their heavy lifting is doing more to benefits shareholders rather than themselves. Much more. Which is why I regard this hazing of the younger adults as a form of indentured servitude, even slavery.

And as I wrote in the chapter on "Congruence" in "How To Survive Your Childhood Now That You're An Adult," being authentic is contingent upon the congruence between who you know in your heart of hearts you should be and being that person. And if you want to be happy, your best shot at it is to be authentic. If you want to be authentic then you must muster the personal integrity to listen to the information that the universe is providing you, "Own Your Life," and manifest the tools to be that person and live the life you know you were born to live. Not the life your parents, teachers, legacy media or social media told you to live. Following someone else's recipe for happiness is a sure-fire way to misery. "Follow your bliss" is Joseph Campbell's updated version of "Follow your dharma" from the Bhagavad Gita. Dharma on the macro level is how the universe is operating; dharma on the micro level is how you as an individual relate to the universe. Or as I enjoy asking my students, "What the fuck are you doing on planet earth for the extremely brief time that you are alive???" This question is usually particularly pertinent to 22-30 year-old adults who - unbeknownst to them - will change jobs 4-5 times during that period.

So maybe you studied marketing for four years at university, went way into debt, took a job at a prestigious company and after a year or two were completely burnt out. This is normal. And you will quit only to rapidly be replaced by some other debt-ridden slave who will work 100 hours per week until they get burnt out. Rinse, repeat. We live in a system of oppression and exploitation, which is why corporations are obviously against unions and anyone standing for workers' rights.

And 99% of us - including myself - are hypocrites. Because I have sympathy for Amazon warehouse workers and drivers urinating into bottles because they aren't allowed to take bathroom breaks, and yet I still want my cat food and guitar strings developed the next day. A system has been established for all of us to get dopamine hits every second. Instant gratification takes too long. But somebody somewhere had to get out of bed at 4am to make those donuts or drive the fresh produce to Whole Foods or toilet paper to Costco, or all of the other luxuries that we now consider to be "normal." Think about the common practice of ordering your lunch to be delivered so that you take 10 minutes instead of one hour off from work so as to recharge your ability to tackle the next task: you take your 10-minute break to swallow your $75 Uber-Eats sandwich and then go right back to producing those widgets that will make other rich people even richer.

The system has been corrupted. And unfortunately the progressives in our country are too weak to make substantive, systemic changes. That is the reason that we are en route to a violent revolution, just like Karl Marx predicted. I have many clients in their twenties who - in addition to their oppressive jobs - seem to be spending an inordinate amount of time in front of screens watching numbers rise and fall next to words such as "Net Worth" or "Bitcoin" or "NFT" or some other word that didn't exist at this time yesterday. This sounds to me both anxiety provoking and depressing at the same time. Very Orwellian. Watching numbers bounce up and down on a glass screen appears to be another form of enslavement, or at least induced complacency - however, the result is that the willing participants end up wired & tired.

Living a balanced life means carving out time to sleep the proper amount of sleep your body needs, eat what your body needs to be energized, get the proper amount of physical exercise to keep your body and mind in shape, and have enough communal time so that your soul is nourished and inspired. As I wrote in "How To Survive Your Childhood Now That You're An Adult," "Mirror neurons do not fire via text message" and "One hug equals one million Facebook likes." All of us need to decrease our screen time, get out in nature, and rejuvenate. My clients who spend hours and hours per day playing video games shouldn't wonder why they are wired & tired. I tell them to go to concerts (not to video the performances on their phones but to experience the music), go to museums (not to take selfies in front of iconic paintings but to wonder what the artists were trying to express), and know that nobody on his or her deathbed ever said, "I should have worked more." Many people have been heard to utter, "I should have LOVED more." "I want to be a human being; not a human doing," is an adage that most of us should have tattooed on our wrists to remind us that nobody wants "Worked Really Hard" on their tombstone.

Our culture suckers primarily 22-30 year-olds into working 100-hour workweeks via "the myth of meritocracy" or what is better known via sociologist Max Weber as The Protestant Work Ethic: work hard and god will reward you. This is a myth. There are so many other contributing factors besides, say, practicing for 10,000 hours. Nepotism, I believe - who you or your family knows - and zip codes are probably better indicators of how someone will succeed or fail over the next fifty years than if you stay in your office until 2am.

Again, all of the things that we consider to be "normal" including going to university and working a 40-hour work week as well as "the nuclear family" should be questioned. All systems have been corrupted and we're amidst rampant erosion of the ground we have been standing on since the industrial revolution. The end of this book will argue that it is time to create a new society, a society not based on survival of the fittest, scarcity-modeled zero-sum game, competition, bottom lines and inequity. A new system that isn't based on oppression and exploitation - especially exploiting the seemingly boundless energy of newly minted adults. And the time to do so is today. Before the planet hemorrhages our little species of thinkers off of it with tsunamis, fires, tornadoes, hurricanes, plagues, diseases, undrinkable water and unbreathable air. If there is any benefit to be gleaned from the most recent pandemic, it is that all of our systems have become corrupted, the old paradigms are moribund, and it is up to us to create a new way of interacting based on love instead of fear, on compassion rather than competition.

So instead of swiping their devices to check their portfolios this morning, younger adults should ask what tremendous, life-enhancing, beautiful, compassionate, new idea or artwork or song or technology is waiting to enter the world through them? Nobody was put on earth to labor in order to make other rich people richer. Newly minted adults who just graduated college need to learn their callings as soon as possible and try to find jobs that facilitate the highest expression of their creative abilities. So long as an adult has enough money to subsist, any job that is only done for the sake of earning more money and doesn't fulfill the person's purpose, will end up causing depression.

Autonomy and agency: being able to decide on the life you want to lead and then making it happen, living your purpose, is what we need to foster and encourage as a society.

In addition, after graduating college, younger adults must find or create their new adult support systems or tribes. Usually 22-30 year-olds meet new people at work and then begin to commune with these people outside of the office. So pursuing a career that will help you surround yourself with like-minded people who are following their purposes will inspire and empower you. Trapped in a cubicle subconsciously competing with ten wired & tired indentured servants staring at computer screens will only lead to a life of pharmaceuticals - especially if you know that one of you will be fired at the end of the year. Did you ever see those experiments with rats in cages?

This is the huge conflict I see in many 22-30 year-olds: they want to impress their bosses and climb the ladder to success so they end up working too many hours and forget to lead balanced lives. In going to the gym or on hikes or to yoga classes or painting classes or other social events they will meet like-minded people and create post-college friendships. This is also a huge correlate to happiness: to have a support group of people with whom you do not work or do business. Many of those blurry lines between business colleagues and friends end up exploding later on down the line.

22-30 year-olds need to have time to make friendships outside of work. More on that in the next chapter on relationships.

Chapter 3. First Relationships, 20-30 years-old

Just think about it for a second: 4 years of being surrounded by 10,000 to 50,000 alcohol and drug fueled humans with very little supervision. Statistically that is why college is often regarded as the happiest times in people's lives. There are so many age-appropriate people to hang out with and so many new and fun activities... I mean, it's difficult to believe that any studying gets done at all!

Currently there are very few courses in our educational system on how to have healthy, loving, supportive romantic relationships so there's a great deal of grasping in the dark for younger adults, most of it fueled by alcohol and drugs. When I was in my 20s - when dinosaurs ruled the earth - we did not overtly have a "hook-up" culture. Of course, there were a few feminists who might knock on your door at odd hours but....

OK let's gently discuss feminism and romance and what I feel are the real problems regarding primarily heterosexual romantic relationships for adults 22-30. And please note that I am an ardent feminist and believe that women should be paid the same amount for the same jobs as men.

On the other hand, I do believe that men have somehow tricked women into believing that they not only can but should act like men sexually, but that they are biologically equal or at least similar to men. However, to the best of my knowledge, women have one ovum that is fertilizable 3-6 days per month and do not require an orgasm to become impregnated; men have billions of sperm cells floating around their testicles most of the time and DO need to have an orgasm in order to fertilize an egg. That's all that I remember from the biology class forty years ago.

According to a 2021 article in The Atlantic, we are amidst a sex recession; the flows of the sexual revolution are ebbing; intercourse as recreation is receding from our crazybusy lives. People in 1st world countries are making the beast with two backs less and less. If this is the case, then I believe that there are five main reasons why people are having less sex:

1. Too much confusing foreplay due to technology.

After a hard day of wielding iPhones like lightsabers, people are all foreplayed out. People are having less sex because most interactions on our mobile devices are subconscious exercises in power. ACCEPT-ed or DECLINE-ed. LOVED or UNLOVED. Ten DECLINEs in a row and your brain tells you that you are UNLOVABLE.

Mobile phones empower everyone including the impotent. But it is all foreplay. And after a day of foreplay people are tired of all of the accumulated rejections, abandonments, denials and betrayals. The impotent feel powerful when they DECLINE calls, when they GHOST you. They showed you who is in control, who is in charge! Each DECLINE, each swipe releases endorphins like a tiny orgasm. Now every imposter suddenly has the ability to instantly FUCK YOU and inform you that his or her time on planet earth is more important than yours. DECLINE! (Tiny orgasm!)

Similarly, the Internet has made pseudo (i.e., delusional) "Public Figures" or ersatz "celebrities" out of a substantial number of talent-challenged narcissists. Hence, it appears as if EVERYONE WANTS AND EXPECTS TO BE PURSUED (as if s/he were a real celebrity) BUT NOBODY WANTS TO BE STALKED (as if s/he were a real celebrity). A conundrum. And here's one of many double standards: ladies, if you want something then go for it, make that shit happen! Men, if you want something… well, I am sorry but you're a stalker.

2. Women are tired of being sexually harassed and sexually assaulted.

I don't live in one of those African or Eastern European countries where marauding militias rampage through a town raping and pillaging everything in sight. However, sexual harassment and sexual assault statistics in America are staggering (AND I believe that most still go unreported). Women live in constant fear. They are objectified by men in the media and in real life. They perpetually feel unsafe. In our society we are not taught how to interact compassionately with members of the opposite sex. We are taught to use them as if they were commodities that can be divorced and deleted as soon as they stop providing.

Men are even sometimes taught that women are shrews that need to be tamed. Thankfully, this subconscious narrative is dying as I discuss in the chapter on "The Myth of Romance" in "How To Survive Your Childhood Now That You're An Adult." I write about the possibility that all great passions in literature as well as real life (see Alain de Botton's "Romanticism" video on

YouTube) are hierarchical, illicit and ultimately dysfunctional. Is titillation possible without even a hint of exploitation?

On average, men are physically larger than women and men are more often in positions of power; females, until 30–40 years ago, were mostly relegated to sexy servile service positions in restaurants, bars, banks, schools, stores, and on airplanes, while men did the "real" business of investing in stocks, working forklifts, traveling to the moon, earning boatloads of money playing professional sports, directing movies, producing records, etc. This is changing and more women are becoming CEOs and running businesses; however, what are the ramifications of gender business equality in our bedrooms?

The elusive "chemistry" that we all seek and crave… could it depend on hierarchy, a power difference, some mysterious "other" like disparate social classes (cf. "Pretty Woman") that must be overcome? Why do basketball players and rock stars have unlimited access to sex? What are women thinking when they line up backstage or in hotel lobbies to shake their money-makers for alpha-male basketball players or musicians?

3. The #MeToo movement.

The #MeToo movement is the best thing to happen to America since the Civil Rights Movement. We need transparency, we need authenticity. We need to eradicate exploitation. We need to make the workplace safe for everyone. Yet the #MeToo movement has made cowards of men — and rightfully so. A mere accusation can destroy both a social and a professional life forever.

A sexual assault accusation makes a man indefinitely unemployable. And it's virtually indefensible. She said, he said. Thus, some men do not wish to risk going to jail, being thrown out of school, being shunned for life and have become gun-shy.

For the workplace, although it does not seem to be occurring, it appears that we need laws to govern how people interact to make women feel safe, to eliminate sexual harassment and people (mostly men) using positions of power to take advantage of people with less power. Healthcare professionals such as psychotherapists cannot legally interact socially with our clients for two years once we see them professionally. It's actually a crime. Specifically, "engaging in sexual relations with a client, or a former client within two years following termination of therapy, soliciting sexual relations with a client, or committing an act of sexual abuse, or sexual misconduct with a client, or committing an act punishable as a sexually related crime, if that act or solicitation is substantially related to the qualifications, functions, or duties of a psychotherapist…" is punishable by revocation of licenses, imprisonment, and fines. Why don't we have laws like this in other industries? Would there be as many abuses of power, men coercing women into sex, if we had laws against fraternization for co-workers?

4. Porn is free, ubiquitous, and hassle-free.

Listen, you're going to have to talk to most sex partners IRL. And by talk… I mean listen. Your sex partner is going to have emotions. At certain times, his or her body may smell quite funky. There might be excess flesh or a blemish somewhere.

Wrinkles. Freckles. Some misplaced hair or lack thereof. A mangled toe or toenail. An asymmetrical nostril. An ear. S/he might not act out your favorite fantasy on every occasion. You might actually have to care about a fellow human being. Well, all of those sticking points vanish into the ethers thanks to pornography! Voila! A visual partner who will do everything your eyes could desire! There's little downside to a private wank — no drama, no hassle, no complaints. A quick rub and you're right as rain. The greatest invention since... uhhhhh... the myth of romantic love.

On the other hand, porn creates unrealistic expectations for one's IRL sex life, so... in the long run it's not actually ideal for your interpersonal relations with other humans. As I wrote in my "How To Survive Your Childhood Now That You're An Adult", nobody watches pornography and thinks, "Oh that's so sweet! They really love each other!"

5. In the 2020s, dating and mating rituals fall somewhere between obsolete and dead. Because rendezvouses have become amorphous and unstructured and there are no agreed upon customs anymore, dating is officially dead. As Nietzsche wrote, "the greatest labour of human beings hitherto has been to agree with one another regarding a number of things, and to impose upon themselves a law of agreement — indifferent whether these things are true or false." Since the gender roles are now fluid, there is no clearly delineated way to know who holds the door open, who pays the check, who decides what activity the couple shall partake in or not partake in. And I know you're thinking, "This is bullshit! All people have to do is talk and agree on who

pays for dinner or who schedules the outing" but IRL people have expectations - and many of those expectations are actually subconsciously ingrained. The map is not the territory, meaning that my understanding of a "date" probably differs from your understanding of a "date." Do your dates include goodnight kisses? It depends. Do your dates end with the wealthier person paying for dinner or do you believe that the man should pay? It depends. Do your Friday evening dates end on Monday morning? It depends. Face-to-face communications about dating and gender roles do not flow as swimmingly as one would imagine. Discussing the most common instruments of power — money and sex — is often quite awkward. And unsexy. In fact, in my workshops I claim that if you analyze most divorces you will find that couples frequently divorce because of disagreements about two fundamental subjects: money and sex. Both are instruments of power.

All of this is to say that we are living in extremely confusing times where impeccable, compassionate and authentic communications are the only way to navigate through the minefields of what is left of "romance." Thanks to the #MeToo movement many men have been dissuaded from pursuing women lest they are outed as sexual harassers; courtship has entered uncharted waters and we are all going to have to learn to uplevel our communication skills in order to avoid mis-expectations. And how many generations will it take for women to transcend slut-shaming? 90% of females I see on Tinder have "Not here for hook-ups" in their profiles. IT'S A FUCKING HOOK-UP APP! It's like me going to Whole Foods and saying, "Not here for shopping." I haven't checked but I am fairly certain that dear few men on Grindr have "Not here for hook-ups" first thing in their profiles.

Women today like to think of themselves as sexually empowered... yet many still appreciate being pursued rather than pursuing... but they don't want to be stalked or hunted like prey... they want men to be chivalrous and do knightly things like buy them drinks and meals as signs that men are providers and protectors... but they do not want men to be macho to the point of rapey (unless the women are total submissives, but then how did they learn to be submissive?)... and above-all, women still cringe at the thought of their friends or anyone calling them "slut." How can we correct this? It all sounds rather confusing.

As opposed to the current "What's in it for me?" transactional manner in which many people interact in our society, as the loneliness and alienation of our lives with porn grows worse, it is time to rethink the power dynamics of contemporary relationships and teach courses that help people be as authentic, loving, compassionate, and altruistic as possible.

The famous line from the film "City Slickers" many years ago was, "You don't understand: women need a reason to have sex; men just need a place." Somehow over the last 20-30 years men have convinced some women that they no longer need a reason to allow someone to penetrate their orifices and that they should be as hedonistic as men. This works for some young adults both male and female who are "setting them up and knocking them down" in contrast to Robert Putnam's "Bowling Alone." Tinder and other "hook up" sites, in terms of percentages, don't bode well for loving long-term relationships. And when Esther Perel states, "How can you desire what you already have?" and there are 400,000 faces to swipe within 15 miles of wherever you are, settling down with one of those faces seems like settling.

In addition, I believe that for the male members of the species, the subsequent bragging to a buddy about your latest seed-spreading conquest is actually an integral part of having sex for the male ego. There is a joke that goes like this: The most beautiful woman in the world and an average man are stranded on a desert island without any hope of ever being rescued. One day the beautiful woman turns to the man and says, "I'll let you have sex with me if you promise never to tell anyone."

The man thinks for a moment and then replies, "What would be the point???"

Women, on the other hand, are still the victims of rampant slut-shaming and I truly believe that if most people learned that a woman had 500 sexual partners, they would not regard the woman in the same way if a man had told them that he had 500 sexual partners.

We have all been taught the wrong things about human sexuality: whether you like it or not, whether you agree or not, your subconscious has been trained to regard other people as objects. Objects that can be used to bring you some form of physical and/or psychological pleasure. This is the "hook-up" culture, which seems much more prevalent amongst 22-30 year-olds then other age groups. "Hooking up" has diminishing returns. Rampant chlamydia, herpes, syphilis, gonorrhea, an occasional unwanted pregnancy. It turns out that "free love" isn't so free for most people. (Although the HPV vaccine should be considered a miracle.)

Anyhow, navigating romantic and sexual relationships for 22-30 year-olds appears to be extremely treacherous. Many 22-30 year-olds have not yet learned how to be emotionally vulnerable and available - they are too busy being stylish and cool; some were so traumatized by ugly previous experiences (mostly drunken, mostly in college or high school) that they have sworn off sex; many angry young men have been so frequently rejected that they consider themselves to be "involuntarily celibate" i.e., "Incels." All of this should be viewed as an EDUCATIONAL problem. And unfortunately there is still much shame around talking about sex and romance that locker room braggadocio, drunken fumbling, and pornography is how too many young people learn about sex.

As brilliant theoreticians such as Robert Johnson, Esther Perel, and Alain de Botton readily discuss, 21st century Western civilization abides by a particular paradigm regarding romantic love. All of these people and I owe a debt to Denis de Rougement who wrote "Love in the Western World" essentially claiming that what we considered to be "normal" regarding romance is esoteric to Western culture and only around 800 years old. It is based on the myth of Tristan and Isolde who have unbridled lust for each for a limited time before Isolde marries Tristan's uncle. The lust is contingent upon the fact that it is illicit - she is already betrothed to someone else.

If you look at America in the 1950s ("Mad Men") and the hierarchical nature of our workforce - women earn less than men for the same jobs - in terms of genders our society is hierarchical, with men both metaphorically and physically on top most of the time. Even through the 1980s most secretaries, food servers, bank tellers, airline stewards, etc. were sexualized (objectifiable) females. Gender roles have changed drastically over the past 20 years but I still wouldn't call them equal or even healthy. There is something to be said regarding consensual hierarchy in the bedroom; the problem is that when hierarchies are endemic throughout a society it is tantamount to systemic prostitution, i.e., casting couches, etc. The #Metoo movement has eliminated many of the Harvey Weinsteins and Bill Cosbys that dominated the entertainment business for the last 100 years, but more regulations and even laws are needed to ensure that women truly feel 100% safe in the workforce.

As I wrote, in "How To Survive Your Childhood Now That You're An Adult," if you and I fixed up two 30 year-old UCLA graduates who both worked in tech, earned $85,000 per year, loved volleyball and yoga and backpacked through South America after graduation, after their date they would report back to us, "S/he is great! There was just no chemistry." For many years I have been exploring the possibility that all great passions are based on mutually complementary psychological and emotional dysfunctionalities. Without hierarchy - one person in a more powerful position than the other in some way - I have found that there is little "chemistry." Thus, as the above-mentioned authors discuss, in the West we get married for the wrong reason - because of this elusive thing that women refer to as "chemistry" but men usually refer to in many other ways. And 800 years ago this system worked because the average lifespan was 28. But now that we know that lust fades and we are living until 87, marriage for life is an abominably stupid idea.

And the only remedy - as Alain de Botton so astutely states in his lectures on romanticism - is to be keenly aware of your own craziness (emotional dysfunctionality) and to tell your prospective partner, on the first date, how you are crazy. Because they are going to find out sooner or later so it may as well be sooner. And by "crazy" I would translate that into "What is your attachment style?" Do you securely and easily attach to romantic partners, are you trustworthy and assume that other people are trustworthy, or are you suspicious and possibly even self-sabotage because you can only insecurely attach to other people? Or maybe you attach TOO easily and are co-dependent, meaning that you allow your emotional life to be tethered to that of your partner. More on attachment styles later.

Aside from being aware of and laying out our personal psychological afflictions for our potential mates, 22-30 year-old young adults should learn if the person sitting across the table from them has similar interests and priorities. All of this is done through "talking," something younger adults have become seriously deficient at. Nine times out of ten when a 22-30 year-old says they were "talking" to their partner it means that they were texting. Then I have to explain to them that 93% of communications are non-verbal, mirror neurons do not fire via text message, and that texting is a slightly less efficient means of communicating than morse code, smoke signals and cave paintings.

So the vast majority of 22-30 years with whom I speak about relationships - and I admit that a psychotherapy office attracts a skewed population - do not possess the tools to have healthy adult romantic relationships. Their expectations are unreal, technology is a huge disservice to them, and some are so emotionally desperate and bereft that I have to send them to Co-Dependent and or Love Addicts Anonymous meetings immediately just so that they can get out of bed and feign a semblance of adult life.

"The first cut is the deepest" sang Rod Stewart in 1976 and whenever you experience that first love, whether it's in high school, college or later, whenever you break up (and the percentages are fairly high that you will not live happily ever after with your first love), it will probably sting the most of all of your break-ups. There's a sense of despondency and hopelessness that accompanies the endings of many first love affairs that I have rarely seen elsewhere. Thus, for many young adults 22-30, who are individuating from their parents, possibly living alone and working full time for the first time, the death of their first love is usually both traumatic and dramatic. Again, the faults lie with our educational system and the media, both legacy and social. Driving into the sunset in a film implies that the happy couple has traversed all obstacles to being together and will live happily ever after. "There's no 'Pretty Woman 2'." It's actually the transcending of impediments and obstacles that helps couples bond together.

So it seems as if most relationships for 22-30 year-old young adults are doomed from the start. They may be fun and exciting for some time. They are probably excellent learning opportunities as these freshly minted adults try to accommodate other freshly minted adults into their lives during their peak labor years, but most of them will end in pain due to the fact that many people subconsciously equate dysfunctionality with love; thus, they subconsciously sabotage their relationships and make them dysfunctional, because this dysfunctionality was modeled by their parents when they were young. Conflating arguing and confrontation with "love" seems to be at epidemic proportions today: the relationships of "soulmates" - those of great passion - I often refer to as relationships of "fucking and fighting."

Another note regarding dysfunctionality: whatever qualities you love about a person when you meet them, you will hate them for in the end. My psychotherapy supervisor recounted a story of a couple that was getting divorced and came to see him. He asked them what they liked about each other when they got married. The wife said, "I liked the way he chose the restaurants and made decisions." The husband said, "I liked the way she made me laugh."

"Why are you getting divorced?" asked my supervisor.

"He's so controlling!" she bellowed.

"All she does is make fun of me!" he cried.

What you love someone for in the beginning of a relationship, you'll hate them for in the end.

As an observation please allow me to note that over the past 15 years in private practice as a psychotherapist I have heard scores of women upon dissolution of their marriages claim that their husbands were narcissists. I refrain from asking, "Did you not notice this while you were creating your many children and homes with him or is this a rare case of late-onset narcissism?" If a man falls in love with a woman because she is adventurous, in the end he will say that she was borderline (as in Borderline Personality Disorder). If a woman falls in love with a man because he makes reservations at restaurants and orders great wine, in the end she will say that he was controlling and narcissistic.

I have little to say about Borderline Personality Disorder other than I disagree with the DSM that it is a personality disorder and believe that these people simply have poor tools (extreme emotional reactions) in order to try to gain attention as well as love and affection. These qualities make them exciting and adventurous at the beginning of relationships; however, there are usually diminishing returns on this level of excitement and after a while this type of behavior just seems crazy. Exciting in the beginning, borderline at the end. Same behavior; different times.

To conclude, 22-30 year-olds - in general - are terrible at relationships. **They don't know what they really want and don't have tools to get what they really need. It's a horrible situation that often ends with a waft of unnecessary drama and**

trauma. We need courses to teach people how to authentically and compassionately express not only their wants and needs but their boundaries. Until communications - and I mean face-to-face in a well-lighted room, not texting or DM-ing or emailing - are normalized, the quality of relationships will continue to decline until these people "bottom out" and then either become reclusive avoidants or decide to "lean in" to a new set of authentic and compassionate tools so that they can lovingly express their vulnerability and inspire their romantic partners to do the same.

Chapter 4. Careers, 30-45 years-old

In contemporary Western society, when strangers meet for the first time, they usually first ask three questions to discern if the other person is a friend or foe:

- What's your name?
- Where are you from?
- What do you do (to earn a living)?

Human beings are tribal in nature and now that we live in cities we still check to see if strangers are members of our tribe or not. Ira Israel and Esther Goldberg would know from their names that they are members of the same tribe - literally. Xi Jinping and Christina Whitman would have to dig deeper to find commonalities. Being from the same plot of land would imply that you were members of the same tribe; hence, names from a thousand years ago often described locations such as "de la Montagne" (from the mountain) or "du Jardin" (from the garden). And then the names shifted 6 or 700 hundred years ago from signifying places to signifying occupations. "Goldsmith" was someone who worked with gold; Harvey Carpenter, Bob Farmer, etc.

But when family names started to identify with work, work also took on a new meaning in people's lives. "I am a doctor" is very different than "I earn my living working as a physician." So now we are faced with the real problem in our society now that we are no longer tribal and territorial: it is the problem of personal identity. For the past few generations, laborers identify with their work and that's the transition from job to career.

Again, "I'm a lawyer" sounds alot different than "I earn my living practicing the law." "I'm an entrepreneur..." etc.

Yes, there's usually a certain stability attained when people's jobs transmute into putative careers, something seemingly more permanent. But these careers also have pitfalls such as golden handcuffs.

For people of my generation, this transition from job to career and from renting to buying a home usually occurred for people in the age group of approximately 30-40 year-old adults living in urban and suburban areas. They settled down with a romantic partner, moved in together, got engaged, earned more money than they thought they would ever earn, paid off any credit card debt and student loans, possibly bought an adult sofa and expensive bed, went on their dream vacations to Hawaii, Paris, Greece, Machu Picchu and/or the latest trendiest Caribbean destination, and checked a few things off of their bucket list...

This could also be seen as reaching a "level of mediocrity" where you can ease off of the pedal and stop being so wired & tired. People often lose their drives and become complacent - usually because they climbed their way up some imaginary ladder and are earning more money than they thought they would earn, have attained some level of putative "success" after being exploited for most of their 20s, or have just plain given up.

In particular, homeownership - signing up for 30 years of debt known as a mortgage - seems to induce pride in many 30-40 year-old adults - it gives them a sense of accomplishment, a sense of arrival. Homeownership in our society appears to represent having accomplished true "adulthood" - when you invite your own parents over for dinner in your new house (that is more expensive than their house) and show off your adult appliances like washers and dryers, lawn sprinkling systems, alarm systems and electric garage door openers. Your parents are very proud of you and the investment they made in your education. It all worked out. You succeeded. You can live happily ever after. You have won!

What I am discussing here are the mostly subconscious "If... then..." tacit agreements that society duped us into believing during our teens. For example, "If you go to a good school, you will get a good job." "If you work hard, you will be successful." "If you are successful, you will earn boatloads of money." "If you earn alot of money, then you will be able to buy "capital" (property, house(s), car(s)) and OWNING things is what adults do." "If you OWN alot of cool shit, then people will like you." "If more people like you, then you will have a wider selection of more desirable mates." "If you have a larger selection of desirable mates then, you will be able to choose the brightest and finest and nicest and richest mate, buy alot of shit, and live happily ever after." Immediately you can see the problems with this formula but if you look at all of the television shows, films, operas and all of the social media that floods our lives, you will see that this "American Dream" formula is still flourishing. So it's not exactly a level of mediocrity that I am discussing here; it's more like a homeostasis, it's more like the rewards and lifestyle that you attain for reaching your level of mediocrity that are being discussed in this chapter.

The major questions that you need to ask yourself are, "Where did I learn what my measure of success was? What is lurking around my subconscious as the trophy of 'winning'?" Did you spend your twenties aiming to hit certain markers such as "Manager" "Director" "Partner" or calling yourself a "Founder" "Entrepreneur" or "Public Figure" on LinkedIn and Instagram? Are you subconsciously competing against one or both of your parents, an older sibling, the mean girl from high school, or the bully from grade school? How did you learn what it would mean for you to be successful? And how much of what you have supposedly accomplished was done out of spite? Were your dreams of being an artist, writer, musician, or dancer stomped out of you when you and your parents started paying $50,000 for you to go to college? You were going to join the Peace Corp or Teach America but...

Please allow a slight digression while I make a distinction between "the Gig Economy" in contrast to the old legacy system of 9-5 employment with benefits. I make this distinction because as mentioned above it relates to personal identity which - due to the way the gig economy is intertwined with social media - should include a brief discussion of not-so-latent narcissism in our society. If you have an old fashioned, old school, old economy "job" in an office with health insurance and retirement benefits, then you can skip ahead. However, if you are part of the new "gig-economy" the below critique may resonate with you. Or make you cringe. My intention here is to raise consciousness around the inauthenticity that the Internet appears to have fomented and engendered. Personally, when I look on social media I see a teeming parade of fetid hawkers.

Let me please ask you, when was the last time you asked a child what he or she or they wanted to "be"—or rather "have" as an occupation—when he or she or they grow up and he or she or they replied,

"When I grow up I want to be an international keynote speaker!"?

Or, "When I grow up I want to be a public figure!"?

Or, "When I grow up I want to be a life coach!"?

Or, "When I grow up I want to launch an online summit!"?

Or, "When I grow up I want to be a visionary!"?

Or, "When I grow up I want to be a blogger!"?

Or, "When I grow up I want to be a self-published author!"?

Or, "When I grow up I want to be an urban shaman!"?

Or, "When I grow up I want to be a Zen priestess!"?

Or, "When I grow up I want to be a spiritual advisor!"?

Or, "When I grow up I want to be a guru!"?

Never, that's when. Because until extremely recently these were not considered to be professions or occupations. And most of them still are not. Most of them are punchlines. But because there are few barriers to entry in the new gig-economy—a jaunt to the local library to use a public computer if you cannot afford a mobile phone—many worker-bees are marketing themselves as queens. "Fake it until you make it" is their mantra as they announce to the world that they are now an internationally famous "Public Figure" on Instagram and TikTok. How would you reply if your child looked up at you and said, "Mom, dad, I'm going to make the world a better place and earn a living by posting new-age clichés and spiritual truisms on Instagram and TikTok"? Self-publishing a book about overcoming your challenging child-hood in Greenwich Connecticut using binaural beats does not make you a psychologist. Posting blogs on tarot cards or astrology or psilocybin doesn't make you an expert; it just means that you're probably yet another self-entitled trustafarean trying to as-suage your white-privilege guilt by living in a yurt in Topanga Canyon and littering TikTok with inconsequential and unedu-cated opinions.

The problem is that people in the gig-economy create fic-tional careers on the Internet in order to look successful (hence narcissism), and then must be somewhat congruent with these fictions in real life. But it's impossible. And this hypocrisy and outright lying eats at these influencers' souls. Just like earning money on bitcoin does: because you are not doing anything to benefit society or fellow humans. Marx predicted that workers would become alienated if they couldn't enjoy the immediate fruits of their labors. Bitcoin has existed for 14 years and has less applications than a dishrag. Right now Bitcoin is just gambling. There's no labor. It's guessing. There's dear little skill involved. On any given day half of the bettors will be right and half will be wrong. One may as well flip coins all day. This is a fiction that erodes its author. Maybe Jaron Lanier is right? Maybe we need to remake the Internet? Maybe some regulations or barriers to entry would clean out the festering cesspool of charlatans clogging up the bandwidth 6 seconds at a time? The gig economy plus busy-ness-media equals teeming parades of fetid hawkers. And many of these 30-40 year-olds suffer from the imposter syndrome seeing as they know first-hand that their lives are not as joyful as what is represented on social media.

We can clearly see that the underlying foundation of capitalism coupled with continuous disingenuous "marketing" on the Internet has caused at least one or two generations of Westerners to grow up inauthentically. These millennials and gen-y people worship false icons. How can they not know that these TikTokers and Instagramers lead horrible - albeit beautifully air-brushed - lives. How could two generations of people devote hundreds of hours per week to making Mark Zuckerberg and a handful of other aspy white guys richer? Please forgive the above rant on people anointing themselves as famous before they actually accomplish anything; I happen to live in Santa Monica, which is littered with liars, hypocrites, and phonies living off of their parents and grandparents' funds for their entire lives yet feeling obliged to fake some level of notoriety on the no-barrier-to-entry Internet.

On the other hand, many of you worked 100 hours per week at various jobs for most of your twenties and then settled into one of those jobs. Then you bought "capital" (a house, a car, some investments) and now find yourself wearing proverbial golden handcuffs. Meaning that you loathe the actual quotidian tasks of your job but can't afford to leave because you would never earn the same amount of money if you started over in a different job. One main theme of my work is vocation vs. prostitution: if you know your vocation or calling then money doesn't matter - you would find a way to follow your purpose no matter what it entailed. Unfortunately, many people get lured into high-paying jobs that don't nourish their souls or feed their hearts. That would be an example of rising to your level of mediocrity and not being able to afford to live your passion because you enslaved yourself to a 30-year mortgage and two leased Porsches.

So ask yourself: is your career, the way you earn a living, congruent with who you are and what you know you should be doing during your 80 extremely odd years visiting planet earth? Are you successful but don't love your job and suspect that your colleagues wouldn't shed a tear if you were hit by a bus tomorrow? Or are you still doing the daily grind for fear of being fired and losing "everything" (that is, all of the shit like property that you bought during the last ten years)?

According to Sonja Lyubomirsky, only people who know their callings are happy; those who work in jobs or careers just for the money are bound to be miserable, save those few who constructed widely and colorfully balanced lives and go to work for 20-35 hours per week in a Faustian pact to finance the other 50 percent of their spectacular waking hours. I don't know many people like this. You already know the old adage: in Europe people work to live; in America people live to work. Unfortunately, with globalization and competition more people in Western civilization are "working" more hours than ever. However, all of this rampant productivity is not making the world a better place for the majority of our fellow human beings. It's actually making it worse.

Again, existential questions such as "Who are you?" and "What are you DOING during your brief visit to planet earth?" and "How do you get your sense of personal identity?" will help you summarize the main thread of this chapter: personal identity in Western civilization in the 21st century is enwrapped in labor. Questions such as "How are you?" are often answered by "Crazybusy!" That does not describe "how" anyone is. We have conflated doing and being. You can pull them apart with the mantra "I want to be a human being; not a human doing." Nobody wants "Was Crazybusy" or "Worked Really Hard" or "Kept Up with the Joneses" on their tombstone. You need to be able to disentangle what your job or career is or how you earn money from your personal identity - because throughout your 20s you probably jumped around through a few jobs and now in your 30s you have settled in for some stability. But there are psychological costs for the trappings in which you inadvertently enrolled yourself.

Chapter 5. Settling Down, 30-45 years-old

OK, so after ten years in the workforce you finally managed some stability and security and have partnered with someone and think it is time to buy a home. For me "The American Dream" meant being a part of a community, having a neighborhood, and feeling safe and secure. But since the 1980s "The American Dream" has come to be associated with owning capital in general and a home and/or investment properties in particular. For aeons a home was someplace that a family lived. It's only relatively recently that real estate became an investment and it is good for you to know how and why this happened. This is a function of an artificial increase in demand due to low interest rates and a dwindling supply.

And existentially, what is this concept of "ownership" to which we are all addicted and which we all consider to be "normal"? Have you ever heard the phrase "You can't take it with you."? I mean, just because some local government has parceled a plot of earth into a specific dimension and in the basement of some city hall lies a deed for that plot… does that mean that you "own" the land? Or does it mean that you have some limited rights to build something on that arbitrarily delineated plot of earth while you're alive? So the concept of "land ownership" and in particular using these plots of earth as investments is relatively recent. Just ask yourself, which is older: the 30-year mortgage or the nuclear family? Do you see what I am saying? As a corollary, please remember that Franklin Roosevelt founded our current system of Social Security starting for people at 65 years old; however, the average lifespan for Americans at that time was 62. Now that we're living until around 80 it's no wonder why the system will soon be bankrupt.

All of these systems - the nuclear family, 30-year mortgage, social security, retirement, etc. - need to be examined now that technology and medicine and other systems have changed exponentially. Let's look at the nuclear family: one premise or assumption of this book is that human beings are tribal. "It takes a village" is a phrase that we have all heard countless times. And yet the nuclear family - especially with a divorce rate of around 50% - doesn't not seem to be optimal. In my community, where I have seen women return to work 6-8 weeks after giving birth, having their child effectively raised by someone else seems suboptimal. I am not sure what the solution is, but there are obvious subconscious ramifications for children whose parents divorce and do not have a firmly established village or tribe to rely on. Children sometimes (actually, often) assimilate fighting and ruptures as "There must be something wrong with ME: if I were perfect then mommy and daddy wouldn't be splitting up." At this time, I know not of any successful communes or kibbutz-like institutions - artificially created tribes or villages - that raise healthy children. But I imagine that over the next 50 years other possibilities than the dominant nuclear family structure will arise.

I've seen Esther Perel discuss how recent it is that couples expect their partners to take out the trash and make travel reservations and walk the dog AND give their partners mind-blowing sex. Previously - even within our own culture - lives were less fluid and more compartmentalized. Compartmentalization was more prevalent in village life. But the real toll taken on people when they settle down is that they often fall into the role of playing psychotherapist for their partner. This is brilliantly described by Harville Hendrix in "Marriage as the Path to Wholeness" when he states that the subconscious purpose of marriage is to enable us to complete our childhood; our parents had deficits (they didn't love us unconditionally), those deficits became defense mechanisms, and those defense mechanisms became our personalities. And we'll always be attracted to people who can re-create the dynamics from one or more of our primary caregivers. Marianne Williamson adds, "If our partners can't replicate those dynamics, we'll train them to replicate those dynamics!"

So it seems as if the nuclear family and broken nuclear families (single parents) create a vicious cycle of wounded people who in our society finally settle down with someone and then subconsciously try to work out (process) their childhood wounds. This is often what I see in psychotherapy sessions with couples. Each partner has expectations that are often some form of compensation for what they DIDN'T receive as a child. And then you add mortgage payments and babies into the mix and it's a recipe for divorce if not disaster.

There's a scene in "Blazing Saddles" where the sheriff holds a gun to his own head and takes himself hostage so that the townspeople do not kill him. Over the course of my fifteen years of practicing psychotherapy, this scene is an apt analogy for what I believe occurs when couples live together - whether married or not: individuals either consciously or subconsciously WITHHOLD affection in order to terrorize their partners into capitulating to meet their supposed "needs" or desires — their "demands." (Please note that I am an ardent feminist and believe that men can also say "no" and need a reason to have sex. I have witnessed men's bodies shut down, i.e., impotence, just as many times as I have witnessed women consciously or subconsciously shutter the nookie factory.) So if living together and marriage has become detrimental to a couple's sex life, I approach the situation as if I am mediating a hostage negotiation. In this case, both parties must articulate their demands and the other party must make their partner feel heard (even if they disagree with the demand or the context in which it is stated).

This is accomplished by what psychotherapists refer to as reflective or active listening:

"So if I hear you correctly… you feel that…"

I believe it is essential to be able to VALIDATE your partner's emotional experience irrespective of what they or their wounded child is saying. Throughout our daily lives when our listeners are multitasking and not matching our facial affects, they are unintentionally invalidating our emotional experiences.

As I said earlier, "Mirror neurons do not fire via text message." In the late 1960s, UCLA professor Dr. Albert Meharabian found that 93% of communication is non-verbal:

7% happens in spoken words

38% happens through voice tone

55% happens via general body language

Which is why I teach couples the techniques of mirroring and matching so that they can sync up, attune, and resonate with each other — and actively VALIDATE their partner's emotional experience, whatever that may be. Sometimes I even have them speak to each other in different languages, to prove to them that they can still attune to each other even if they don't understand the words. Here's the speech I give to couples at the onset of working with them: "Right and wrong are on the other side of the front door: you can pick them up on the way out," I tell couples. "I'm not a judge and you are not attorneys trying a case. Both of you are entitled to whatever emotional experiences you are having and I'm going to teach you how to VALIDATE each other's feelings — even if you cannot understand them or blatantly disagree with them. As Harville Hendrix says, "You can either be RIGHT or you can be in RELATIONSHIP."

So when I find that either person is or both people are withholding physical affection, I treat the situation as a hostage negotiation and coach both parties into actively hearing each other and reflecting back what they hear as accurately as possible both verbally and non-verbally. The ways we communicate through DM, IM, email and texting have profound ramifications and are rife with misinterpretation. In his Masterclass, Chris Voss states that most emails are read negatively. I concur and believe that written sarcasm and irony often land poorly while the intention was friendly or even loving. We have become pawns of technology and I have witnessed it destroy hundreds of loving relationships. So if you are currently living with your spouse or partner and your sex life is not what you want it to be, the first thing I suggest is learning how to make your partner feel heard and then listening to their conscious demands and then possibly working with a couples counselor who can help you understand your partner's subconscious demands - the ones emanating from the wounded child in them. I believe that making your partner feel heard and validating their emotions will inspire them to release the affection that he or she has been holding hostage from you.

As sentient beings the one thing we want above all is to be loved UNCONDITIONALLY. And yet, we only have tools to help us gain love CONDITIONALLY - because we're successful, we speak well, we possess the right status symbols, we vacation in the coolest places, etc. Thus the entire system acts like a Resentment Factory because we can never have what our hearts truly crave.

Reflective listening - empathy - feeling heard and having our emotional experiences validated is the closest we can come to having our emotions validated in our society. This is what therapists are trained to do and this is what I train couples to do. Marriage is not therapy; however, without these tools many partners let their subconsciouses run wild and that usually ends up destroying the marriage. Authentic, compassionate communications are the only solution.

And, of course, you can subconsciously attempt to correct the injustices of the universe by spawning and being the parents to those children that you wished that you had had... ah...to family or not to family. Once you have reaped the rewards of rising to your level of mediocrity and attained some semblance of stability and security in your life, now it's time to decide if you want to have children. I must admit, this is not my area of expertise as I am childfree and have never seriously entertained having children. In all honesty, as a psychotherapist it turns out that the vast majority of my clients happen to be 20-25 years my junior, so I often think of them as my children. But if you are thinking of having children, the common "con" I hear is that of planetary instability due to climate change, humankind's abuse of natural resources such as water, air and land, and political unrest that could lead to civil war, terrorism, world war, and nuclear attacks. Having a child is a huge decision and many people do not truly understand the emotional, psychological and financial commitments that they are making when they decide to have children. The world has changed drastically in the past few generations, so I think it behooves you to make a conscious decision on whether or not you are fit and prepared to be a parent. Because - as I wrote in "How To Survive Your Childhood Now That You're An Adult - parenting is the toughest job in the world.

Chapter 6. Flying High

Living the Dream of Happy American Family Life!

(this page intentionally left blank[1])

---

[1] I agree that as a psychotherapist I see a skewed population, but the joys of family life are usually retrospectively romanticized. Making lunches and keeping small humans from lunging into traffic for 18 years seems to be like jumping one hurdle after another. There is a negative side too.

Chapter 7. Crashing, 45-65 years-old

For a huge swath of inhabitants of Western civilization, eventually a crisis erupts and the illusions of "The American Dream" and the "good life" that were supposed to engender happiness die a smoldering death. Maybe you did everything right: settled into a career and became successful, married your ideal partner and bought a house and some plants, got a dog and then had some children… and then one day it all came crashing down. Often it is the sudden death of a loved one or getting unexpectedly fired from your dream job or a marital infidelity that causes people to rethink their priorities. For me, it is often really an unconscious re-opening of the primal abandonment wound - a wound that is registered as a tremendous cosmic betrayal - that causes a rupture in the illusion (of someone else's definition) of success. You did everything right and then THIS cataclysmic event occurred and shattered your faith, the faith you had in the tacit agreement you made with the universe. This rupture will uncover and reveal your resentments: you gave up your dreams, you gave up your passions, you gave up living a balanced, healthy life in order to abide by the insane societal norm of being crazybusy, which has left you wired & tired. Now you're sick of feeling perpetually stressed and you need it to stop. Through various media you were taught that if you did everything by their prescription that you would be happy. But this rupture has revealed that you're not happy. Thus, you feel betrayed. You kept up your end of the deal: career, house, car, 80-hour work week, marriage, comfy sofa, cool vacations. But it didn't add up to authentic happiness. As Krishnamurti said, "It is no measure of health to be well-adjusted to a profoundly sick society." And in our society being "well-adjusted" probably means that you're wired & tired.

This is usually an excellent time for debilitating panic attacks and depression to overtake you. Your being wired & tired has reached a new level. It has gone BEYOND. Your body might give up, give in. It can no longer muster the strength to place that fake smile on your lips and play the game anymore. Could these panic attacks or this depression be the way that your body is signaling to other people around you - say, your boss or people who depend on you financially - that your soul is unnourished, that you feel like a slave, that you feel trapped in a lifestyle that doesn't bring you joy? Or maybe it's an existential angst that has untethered you from the daily grind - maybe the death of a loved one has caused you to ask yourself, "What does it matter if I have six zeroes or eight zeroes on some computer screen? I don't have the freedom and autonomy to pursue the activities that would nourish my heart and soul."

For a time this phenomenon was referred to a "mid-life crisis" and isolated to diminutive, balding Jewish men who bought Porsches and tried to have affairs with their daughter's friends. But no longer! Thanks to terrorism, war, climate change, natural disasters and pandemics, now these existential crises are available for everyone, anytime!

My existential crisis started at age 18 and lasted quite some time. There's really no other excuse for somebody to spend 25 years studying philosophy, spirituality and psychology - is there? I was fortunate to not succumb to depression. My compensation for the rupture caused by an automobile accident in 1985 was OCD. Here is how I describe it: Something happened. Crushed metal, a crushed leg, a crushed face. It was traumatizing. And my mind said, "That was awful. I'm never going to let that happen again." Then it tried an array of potential solutions to ensure that that traumatic event never occurs again. Now it is 10 or 20 or 30 or 40 years later and that problem and the trauma are long gone but my younger mind's solution still exists. And that "solution" - those compulsive behaviors and obsessive thoughts - has been pathologized and given a name: it is now called an Obsessional Compulsive Disorder. It is a dis-order - although it has not hindered me from living a colorful life. However, as defined by the DSM, orderly minded people do not suffer from OCD. If my mind were ordered correctly or correctly ordered and hadn't compensated for this trauma in this manner, it would not operate like this. We agree that there is no gene that causes people to check their stoves or the locks on their doors hundreds of times before leaving the house—correct? OCD is not something that anyone is born with. It is a reaction. It is your younger mind's best shot at solving a traumatic problem.

When clients come into my office complaining about similar compulsive behaviors or obsessive thoughts, I ask them to assume a meditative posture and then we gently walk their minds backwards until they find when these "solutions" first appeared. Then we discuss what was going in the patient's life at that time and find anything that a young mind might find traumatic—parents' divorce, a betrayal, an abandonment, a fall, the death of a loved one, a supposed failure, a humiliation, a car accident, a loss—and discuss all of the feelings around the event. Then we temporarily secure a narrative (all narratives are dynamic, constantly in flux—you and your mind recount stories about the same incident differently over time) about the origin of the obsessive thoughts and compulsive behaviors. Then I ask a series of absurd, rhetorical questions unequivocally proving that the event and subsequent trauma are long gone and the younger mind's "solutions" are now trying to solve a problem that no longer exists. Finally we create a phrase or mantra that the patient employs whenever the thoughts or behaviors rear their loving heads. Because at some point in time, these thoughts and behaviors - that are now pathologized as OCD - were our young mind's solution to a problem.

So the aforementioned car accident was the rupture and one of my compensations for it was OCD. What was your rupture and how did it change you? A divorce or bad break-up? A death of a loved one? A transportation accident?

- How did it change you?
- How did you compensate?
- How did your relationship with faith and security change?
- Who could you depend on?
- Who showed up for you and who didn't?
- Who told you to buck-up and get back to work?
- Who told you to go to the doctor to get a prescription?

I am not a proponent of "late-onset" depression, OCD, narcissism or many of the other pathologies listed in the DSM. I believe that many of these afflictions are situational compensations and if we removed the situation then the compensation would disappear too. That is why I always try to discern "the inciting incident" (a screenwriting term) that twisted the plot into an unexpected direction and sent the patient down a previously unseen path. Before the car accident, if anyone had told me that I would be writing books and teaching courses on happiness, I would have called them insane.

So now that some rupture has brought to the surface the fact that you are disillusioned, disenchanted, disappointed and discontent, you will need a road map to help you construct a life that will bring you authentic happiness. I suggest that you start by creating a narrative that traces your life hitherto the rupture.

* Who are you?
* How did you become that person?
* Why did you become that person?
* What did you believe?
* What did you hope?
* What did you dream?
* What redemption were you seeking?
* What were the other inciting incidents that occurred?
* What do you think the Universe was trying to tell you?
* What did you secretly hope your parents would say or do?
* What were you trying to achieve?
* Who were you trying to impress?
* Who was the real author of your idea of success?
* What were your truest moments of joy before the rupture?

Then, I suggest tracing times of abandonment, betrayal and disappointment from your earliest memories to date, including times of profound humiliation, shame and embarrassment.

- Is there a pattern?
- How did you react?
- What were your compensations?
- How was your "way of being in the world" shaped by your successes and failures?
- Did you lift weights and become strong to compensate for being bullied as a child?
- Did you become wealthy to compensate for the impotence you felt by not having money as a child?
- Or did you gain alot of weight (subconsciously) so that people could no longer objectify you and violate you physically?
- Or did you become an alcoholic to numb yourself out from painful memories?
- What were your dreams and aspirations when you were at school?
- What led you down the path to become who you are today?

Most importantly, why do you think the shit that you think?

So if your current rupture/crisis is really a re-opening of a core wound of abandonment that registers as a betrayal, it may actually manifest as an underlying feeling of being unlovable, that nobody really cares about you, that you have been no different than a dancing bear for the past 20 or 30 years.

Here are ten things you may feel betrayed by, some thoughts that may be plaguing you:

1. You feel betrayed by the American Dream, which now feels like an albatross of debt (monthly mortgage, school loan & credit card payments) and financial responsibility weighing you down so much that you have little time to do anything but work work work and extinguish one fire after another.

2. You feel betrayed by your romantic partner who you thought would always take care of you, support you through fat and thin, and give you mind-blowing sex (make you feel worthy and desirable) and now seems to have become complacent, can't really be bothered to be continuously sexually adventurous anymore, and does very little to make your life exciting. (Mostly due to the fact that believing that other human beings were put on earth to make your life exciting is commonly referred to as narcissism.)

3. You feel betrayed by whatever success you have attained. You subconsciously learned that if you did all of the right things — earn boatloads of dosh, get married, go on fabulous vacations, crush your 15 minutes of fame or infamy, have the coolest cars and handbags — that you would be happy. Now you are just a miserable automation with closets full of shit, a few cherry-picked glamorous social media photos, and possibly children who want very little to do with you. The moral? The common understanding of the word "success" does not equal happiness.

4. You feel betrayed by your job that has become uninteresting, stupid and boring. However, golden handcuffs have previously kept you from changing careers at this time or pursuing your dreams.

5. You feel betrayed by co-workers and business associates who seemed to take more pleasure in your failures than your triumphs. And now that you are in crisis you find out that they were fair-weather friends.

6. You feel betrayed by your body, which you assumed would not decline as rapidly as a human body declines sitting at a desk or in a car, subway or bus for ten or more hours per day.

7. You feel betrayed by your health, which seems to take tremendous effort — supplements, juices made of dirt, pharmaceuticals, diets, exercise, tofu, sleep — to try to preclude the myriad aforementioned illnesses.

8. You feel betrayed by your government, which is primarily evident to you via taxes and parking tickets, and secondarily in hourly news feeds documenting its jaw-dropping inanity.

9. You feel betrayed by your friends and family members for loving you because you are so gosh-darn positive, feeling compelled to perpetually put your best foot forward in fear of other people abandoning you because you exhibit a wider than acceptable bandwidth of human emotions — such as grief, for instance.

10. You feel betrayed by your parents for loving you conditionally — because you learned how to use toilets and utensils (not simultaneously), learned how to speak a language, learned how to dress yourself, learned how to compete for good grades, learned how to compete at sports, learned how to behave "correctly," learned how to have a good (well-paying) job that enabled you to occasionally snag an attractive sex partner, etc. — when all you really ever wanted is to be loved for being you and being alive. Dancing through hoops like a carnival animal has grown tiresome. You do not want to have to prove anything to anyone anymore.

It appears that the root of the feeling wired & tired could be feeling betrayed by modern life in general, which seems particularly pointless, is punctuated by increasing moments of disillusionment, disenchantment and disappointment and offers you only a modicum of fleeting moments of contentment, probably most often when you are drunk or asleep or both.

Well, welcome to late capitalism!

Welcome to the myth of romantic love!

Welcome to democracy riddled with corruption and bribery!

Welcome to an economic system primarily based on nepotism!

Welcome to a society where passion is usually the result of two (or three or four) people's mutually complementary dysfunctionalities!

Welcome to social media where you compare your complicated inner emotional states with everyone else's glitzy and gilded facades!

Welcome to the information age where you may be penalized for not showing up for 80 hours per week for a job that now actually only takes 4 hours per week thanks to new technology!

Welcome to business for the sake of busyness!

Welcome to disenfranchisement!

Welcome to disenchantment!

Welcome to alienation!

Welcome to unrootedness!

Welcome to modern medicine where everyone suffers from myriad afflictions that can only be remedied by the latest and greatest pharmaceuticals!

Welcome to modern banking where corporations spend most of their time trying to keep you in debt!

Welcome to our highly competitive educational system that teaches that every class has one winner and forty losers!

Welcome to much of modern psychology that addresses mental and physiological symptoms with Band-Aid solutions!

Welcome to continuously feeling WIRED & TIRED!

Maybe it is time to take your autonomy back?

Maybe it's time to re-discover your authentic self and make conscious choices about who you want to be and the lifestyle most propitious to engender happiness?

Maybe it's time to revitalize your life by augmenting your sense of wonder and exploring some of the infinite subjects that you never explored - maybe even never knew existed.

Again, allow me to drive home that many of the aforementioned instances of feelings of betrayal later in life could be re-openings of a primal abandonment wound resulting from being individuated too abruptly - as we do under the "scientific" - what-doesn't-kill-the-little-bugger-makes-it-stronger - paradigm of churning babies into "productive members of society" as quickly as possible. This often results in those intensely productive widget-builders, suicidal gymnasts, extreme sportists, keyboard zappers and screen swipers having INSECURE ATTACHMENT DYNAMICS, always feeling "not good enough," that they will only be happy when they accomplish X, when they summit the next peak, are awarded this trophy, when Bitcoin hits $500,000 (or even $50,000 again), that they are essentially unwhole, imperfect, and that there is perpetually something wrong with them that will be righted when... if... if only...

The brain is the hardware and the mind is the software. Sometime long ago a virus got into your operating system and became a default setting: "I'm all alone. Nobody really cares about me. I'm unlovable," etc. You obviously were not born with this thought nor is there a gene for this trait. And yet during this time of rupture and crashing it is a fundamental paradigm that has led you down some dark alleys. So after wallowing in your own sea of misery for some time, you may realize that you cannot pull yourself out without help. As I already mentioned, I was "on the path" - seeking - for twenty-five years before I started teaching and giving back. It was a highly indulgent time. I am not proud of it. I feel fortunate to have discovered yoga in 1995 and that kept me out of much real trouble as I skipped along from every transformational self-help workshop, retreat, guru and cult leader, at the same time trying to catch-up on the academic material that I missed while at university. I do love learning and that is why I still take various classes every week plus watch an array of university courses online.

At this time of rupture and crisis you may benefit from psychotherapy. Because if you are able to build a rapport with a therapist and share your authentic mental and emotional life, then you should be able to rather quickly develop an understanding of who you are, why you became that person, what that person was hoping to achieve, and the causes and results of the latest blow to your mental paradigm.

I am impatient, so when I see a new therapist, I tell them not to use the front door, not to ask me "And how did that make me feel?" I tell them, "I need you to use the back door - show me what's in my blindspots, show me the stuff I can't see." That is, I believe, what a good psychotherapist will do: gently lead you or lure your mind toward revelations, new ways of envisioning things.

When I work with individual psychotherapy clients in private practice, I usually try to discern and track two major themes:

1. What is the corrective emotional experience that the client is subconsciously yearning for?

2. Who am I showing up as subconsciously for the client? Or, what dynamic or pattern from his or her past are we re-creating with the secret underlying hope of attaining a different outcome this time?

This is a rather dynamic process, a fluid dance, that changes over time as the relationship evolves, but the essential questions remain the same.

The primary therapeutic style I espouse as a therapist is Rogerian, which means that I believe we all want to be loved unconditionally but live in a highly competitive, judgmental society that only enables us to gain love conditionally - by jumping through hoops, getting good grades, becoming wealthy, successful, smart, sexy, etc. - and that psychotherapy provides a safe, nonjudgmental space where clients can process their emotions, "reparent" themselves, and learn to accept and even love themselves without all of the hoops, bells, and whistles. So psychotherapists don't heal anyone, don't fix anyone, and don't cure anyone. Personally, I am extremely resistant to diagnoses and will only provide them when required by insurance companies. Language creates reality. And when someone is branded as having ADHD or Bipolar Disorder or many of the other common moods and behaviors that are pathologized by our culture, it is like a scarlet letter that they usually wear around and use as an excuse for the rest of their lives. Personally I would advise you to shed any former diagnoses and start afresh with new and open ears. For example, most young adults come into my office claiming that they overthink and have been diagnosed with ADHD. Many have been medicated with Adderall, Ritalin, and Vyvanse for over a decade. I ask a few simple questions to deconstruct their paradigms.

"So can you pay attention to something that is enjoyable like making love, playing in the ocean, hang-gliding, being served a 7-course meal at a Michelin restaurant?"

"Yes," they always reply.

And then I explain to them that their minds only fail to pay attention to things that are uninteresting to them. Get it? So instead of medicating yourself in order to pay attention to things that are uninteresting, focus on the things that interest you! Obviously the root of this problem is our antiquated one-size-fits-all educational system that forces all children to take a litany of classes that are wholly uninteresting to them. Then when they complain that they're not interested and they find their mind wandering somebody writes them a prescription so that they focus on the uninteresting material and get good grades.

As previously mentioned, these supposed "failures" in children - being taken to a medical doctor in order to help the child get better grades - are very traumatic and are often assimilated as "I'm all alone. Nobody understands me. There must be something wrong with me. There's something wrong with my brain. I'm different. Life is so easy for other kids - why is it so difficult for me? I guess that I AM ESSENTIALLY UNLOVABLE." And this is - from my experience - how the core wound of so many people in our society manifests. The individuation processes were abrupt and subconsciously registered as betrayals. When parents put their helpless baby in a dark room for 8 hours and let it "cry itself out," that abandonment could be registered as a betrayal by the baby. Then the baby constructs a theory about the world subconsciously such as "People will abandon you; people will betray you" as a defensive mechanism to try to stave off it ever happening again, and then they spend the rest of their lives finding facts that rise to meet that theory. "Y'see, I always knew she was going to cheat on me!" This is one reason why therapy is so valuable: to help you understand your basic operating system: do you inherently believe that the world is a safe and secure place or do you believe that everyone is out for himself and that people will screw you over if you let your guard down. So finding a good therapist is very important to help mirror back to you what is in your subconscious, how you have been programmed, show you what you cannot see without that mirror, and create a safe space so that you can make tweaks and adjustments to help re-program any maladaptive parts of your way of being in the world.

One of my psychology professors at university put it this way, "My job as I see it is to lease my emotions in 50-minute intervals." On the emotional level, this resonates with me because for every "Yes, but…" my clients receive in the "real world" that invalidates their emotional experiences and/or makes them feel "not good-enough," the therapist provides an empathic and supportive "That sounds awful" or "That sounds challenging" or "Awesome!" or "Congratulations!" in order to make them feel secure in whatever emotional experience they are having - especially if they are amidst a crisis or a rupture in their paradigm.

I would say that on the cognitive level contemporary psycho-therapists provide fresh perspectives and help clients "reframe" situations and phenomena so that they are more palatable and acceptable and also to help clients explore new possibilities. In addition, we can provide cognitive-behavioral tools and exercises such as gratitude lists that can help clients expand their under-standings of particular situations and phenomena. Our minds were built to create "woulda-coulda-shoulda-didn'ts" about our pasts and "if xxxxx happens, then I'll be happy" ultimatums about our futures. As Terry Fralich writes, "Suffering equals the reality of now times resistance." So psychotherapists help clients under-stand the past, accept it, and move forward in a positive manner. Stop resisting, stop resenting. Start accepting. Especially shit you cannot change.

Therapy models an authentic, healthy, supportive, intimate relationship for the client; it validates whatever emotional experience the client is having (as long as it is not harmful to anyone including the client); it should help you learn to live in the present moment and release some of the fears and prejudices built from past traumas as defenses to ward off potential future traumas; it could also help you release expectations about the future and cultivate non-attachment to anxiety-causing possible outcomes. In addition, therapists can also provide an array of hands-on, immediate tools like the ones I listed in Chapter 1 in order to help cultivate equanimity and ease and take yourself out of "fight/flight/freeze mode. Ultimately you may learn that you are lovable and through modeling authenticity you should at least learn communication tools that facilitate you getting your emotional needs met. Most people find that there is tremendous liberation in being able to drop their facades and be authentic - even if it's just for an hour per week.

On the cognitive level a therapist can provide fresh perspectives and help you reframe your current situation so that you can either make immediate changes or accept your state of affairs. On an emotional level a therapist can support your authentic desires so that you do not feel like a fraud, an imposter, or a dancing bear about to be whipped for not performing up to the absurd measures of "success" that popular culture (advertising) has indoctrinated you into believing. Thereafter you should be supplied a wide array of tools and practices - the ones that I mentioned in Chapter 1 plus the subjects I believe you should have learned at university listed in the next chapter - on how to regulate your emotions, to find your true vocation/purpose/calling, and create a balanced and healthy adult life.

OK, so there was a crisis, a rupture of your mental paradigm of how reality functions, a disruption of your subconscious faith in "reality" as you knew it, and the tacit agreement you thought you had made with the universe or your religion. And this divorce/firing/accident put into question everything that you considered "normal," and this questioning has led you to seek a greater understanding why you think and feel what you think and feel, which led you to therapy. Awesome! Because once you entertain some new possibilities for who you are and what you're doing during your brief time on planet earth, then you may realize that it is up to you to create an amazing life. Living your life based on someone else's ideal of success was a recipe for disaster waiting for a place to happen - it was only a matter of time. It is this crisis (the same word for opportunity in some languages) that will provoke and inspire you to pull yourself up by your own bootstraps and create the life that you always wanted, the life that will have the best chances for keeping you at the higher end of your happiness spectrum for whatever remaining time you have on the planet.

But before I shift into learning how to pull yourself up by your own bootstraps and employing all of the tools and practices listed in Chapter 1, let me conclude this chapter by discussing the most common rupture that I witness in our culture: divorce. Divorce is rampant in our society - especially for people in the age range 45-65.

Listen, marriage for life was a fantastic idea in the 13th century when the average lifespan was 28 but now that we are living until 85, we obviously need to have renewable marriage contracts, not marriage-for-life contracts. Personally I am in favor of 1-year contracts with options to renew, unless a child is born and then both parents must be committed to supporting said small human until that baby becomes an adult.

Divorce is the second most traumatic event a person can go through - the number #1 trauma being the death of a spouse. But I think divorce can be even more traumatizing because of the way it reopens the primal abandonment/betrayal wound. I mean, you stood in front of 130 of your closest acquaintances as well as the god of your choice and said, "until death do us part."

And here's a compounding reason why many divorces are so painful: because aggrieved partners try to exact dollars commensurate with the betrayal they feel. This is what provoked Rod Stewart to famously say, "Instead of getting married again, I'm going to find a woman I don't like and just give her a house." Because that's how it ends for many men. However, it's often worse for the women. Ironically (from a safe distance, that is), it seems as if some of the husbands were willing to pay millions to attorneys to ensure that the mothers of their children did not get those same millions. I had thought that the opposite of love was indifference, but some of these characters make a strong argument for the opposite of love being hate. The tricks used by the men and their attorneys in these cases also include asking the judges for perpetual continuances at every opportunity. Men still earn more than women and in these cases the husbands had much deeper (albeit often hidden) pockets than their wives so every extra month of proceedings means hemorrhaging the wives' already depleted bank accounts.

When speaking with these traumatized women, it seemed almost inconceivable that they had spent years being courted by, romanced by, married to, making love with, traveling the world with, and making babies with the same men who were now doing everything in their power to crush and destroy them, revenge for reopening the primal abandonment/betrayal wound, in my humble opinion. And I will not even mention how the men tried to pit the children against their mothers (the favorite strategy appears to entail insinuating that the mother is mentally ill), failed to return texts and telephone calls regarding the drop-offs and exchanges of children, and gaslit the women in public (the preferred location to gaslight your wife is apparently at your children's school, in front of all of her friends and your children's teachers). In one case the father even instigated an investigation by Child Protective Services of the mother of his own children. Granted, these women who I have met may be isolated cases, but...

If renewable marriage contracts aren't available by the time I get married, I'd like whatever born-again atheist (thank you, Gore Vidal, for that wonderful phrase) who officiates the wedding to set the bar extremely low, pronouncing something such as: "Dearly beloved, we are gathered here today to join Ira and his beautiful wife in union... Listen, let's be real... it's probably not going to work out. If I were a betting man, I'd bet that in three or four years she will be calling him a narcissistic jerk and he will be telling everyone she is borderline... so let's just have a nice party and enjoy this happy day in each other's loving company... cool?"

But until we replace "marriage for life" with something more sustainable, the best we can do is realize that it's very difficult for two people to evolve together consistently over 50, 60, or 70 years. Interests diverge. People have different priorities. Passion usually dies or diminishes or goes through ebbs and flows. People get complacent and believe that a wedding is tantamount to crossing the finish line when it's actually the beginning of the race. This would be an excellent course to teach younger adults graduating college: What To Expect From Marriage.

If you recently experienced a rupture to your status quo - getting divorced, fired or experiencing the death of a loved one - this crisis may force you to re-evaluate all of your values, interests and priorities.

Chapter 8. Rising from the Ashes

On this perfect day when everything is ripening and not only the grapes are becoming brown, a ray of sunshine has fallen on my life: I looked behind me, I looked before me, never have I seen so many and such good things together. Not in vain have I buried my forty-fourth year today; I had the right to bury it... How could I not be grateful to the whole of my life?

~ Nietzsche, "Ecce Homo"

The primary responsibility of our minds is to keep us safe, secure, and out of harm's way; it does this by taking the traumas of the past and projecting them into the future, simultaneously creating resentments: resentments are when you want something to be different that is impossible to change. I resented that I had scars on my face. Some people resent that their parents got divorced, that they were forced to go to schools they didn't want to go to, that their sibling was supposedly favored by their parents, that they were humiliated or violated or oppressed or molested in some way. "How To Survive Your Childhood Now That You're An Adult: A Path to Authenticity and Awakening" proposed that living bound to our childhood resentments, our initial insecure attachment dynamics, our unforgiveness, our low self-esteem and all of our compensations for childhood traumas was INAUTHENTIC. And our best shot at happiness is to show up authentically, to jettison the false selves we created to survive our childhoods and get our emotional and psychological needs met with the tools of an eight or ten year-old child. I propose a path to authenticity which I believe is relatively simple to understand

and follow, namely Attachment, Atonement, Attunement, Presence and Congruence:

Attachment - being aware of our primary attachment dynamic(s). Do we, like 33% of Mary Ainsworth's babies in her 1969 "Strange Situation" experiment, believe that the world is an inherently safe place and that our mother and primary caregivers would never betray us? Or are we healthily suspicious of strangers and strange situations, keep our doors locked and our passwords hidden away because deep down we know that the world is a dangerous place and that when given the opportunity many people will take advantage of us. Every human, as they are "thrown" in language, develops a paradigm. A baby's crying signals to its caregivers that it is hungry, dirty or tired. Parents have to interpret this crying and meet the baby's needs. But sometimes they get it wrong. Sometimes the parents are smothering. Sometimes the parents are absent. Parenting is the most difficult job in the world and as adults we must be aware of the basic default perceptions of the world and of people that our minds created during our formative years. Human beings are an interdependent species and all of the corrupted competitive systems by which we interact need to be revised or replaced so that people can be vulnerable and compassionate without fear of being exploited or violated.

Atonement - releasing your resentments about things we cannot change. Our minds try to keep us safe by extrapolating the traumas of the past into the future. These are the grudges that we hold onto, the woulda-shoulda-coulda-didn'ts, and our fantasies about "What if...." i.e., "What if I had won the lottery, married

the other person, was 6 inches taller, wasn't in that accident…
then I would be happy!" It's funny how very few people have a
mind that believes that the universe is conspiring in their favor.
Most of the time we fail to grasp the big picture of privileges and
luxuries that we enjoy and instead focus on the traumas that occurred long ago. Atonement - at-onement - means realizing our
essential wholeness and oneness - if it appeals to you, our "divin-
ity" - and then employing the tool of forgiveness in order to clean
up the past so that we can show up authentically for the present.

Attunement - being able to connect with and attune to others. "Mirror neurons do not fire via text message," I am fond of
saying. Text messaging isn't much better than morse code,
smoke signals or cave paintings - it's just a little faster. We need
to be in the same room with the person, feel their energy, see
their whole body, look into their eyes. And if we really want to
connect with another human we must mirror and match their
body language. Shakespeare wrote, "The eyes are the window to
the soul." Even by Zoom and FaceTime much is lost. 93% of all
communications are non-verbal, claims UCLA Professor Albert
Mehrabian. We all need to refine our tools for connecting with
fellow humans. The younger generations who are being brought
up during the pandemic interacting with their peers primarily
through FaceTime and text do not have the best tools to really
interact "IRL" WITH PEOPLE. You'll notice poor eye contact
and that they are easily distracted. Technology has deluded us
into thinking that we're connecting when we actually need much
more. "1 hug equals 1 million social media 'LIKEs'."

Presence - not letting your mind drag you into the past or future. I love the concept of "The Zone." Athletes such as football players or boxers must be extremely present and pay a high price if they allow their minds to meander. I teach one particular form of meditation known as "observing your thoughts" meditation that subtly demonstrates to students that they have a choice whether to listen to the thoughts in their heads or just observe them. Once you understand that you have some control over your thoughts you can discover activities that put you into "The Zone." For me it has traditionally been yoga and meditation, but I have recently discovered swimming, tennis, boxing and biking. These are all individual practices and you need to find the ones that work for you. Being able to be in the present moment - and it may mean taking time to recompose ourselves - to drop the prejudices from our pasts and our fears (of possible humiliation, abandonment, betrayal) of the future is another key aspect to showing up authentically.

Congruence - having your outer world match your inner world or as Andre Gide stated: "It is better to be hated for what you are than to be loved for what you are not." It is a privilege to live in a sophisticated society - not be running from lions and tigers and not scavenging for food and clean water - and be able to decide to have the time to discover your vocation and then design your life so that you can live that calling. If you have this opportunity, then it is your responsibility to find what nourishes your soul and pursue it. If the universe is telling you that your vocation is to be a parent then be the best parent you can be. If you love art or music or literature or dancing then you have to design your life so that you can follow your passions. "Follow your bliss," said Joseph Campbell, which is an update to "Follow your dharma" as stated in the Bhagavad Gita. Dharma on the macro level means "the principles that order the universe." On the micro, or individual, level, dharma means "how we relate to the ordered universe." In other words, what are our vocations? Voco in Latin best translates as "calling." But "callings" do not occur ex nihilo. If we have a calling or vocation, this means something is calling us — right? It implies that we are receiving some information from somewhere that is pointing us in a particular direction.

Being congruent entails writing a list of characteristics you wish to embrace and then having the personal integrity to embrace them. If you are a thief and a liar then you are going to live in a world of thieves and liars. If you are compassionate and altruistic then you will live in a world of compassion and altruism. You cannot be incongruent for very long without the universe speaking to you via a malady, an accident, getting fired, having your spouse leave you, spending time in jail, something unexpected will happen and then twenty years later you will realize that that event, that rupture put you on the path you were supposed to be on all along. For me, this is the way karma operates. It may not be instant and certainly the occurrences of one lifetime cannot be explained by your actions alone in that lifetime but working in conjunction with your soul and what you know in your heart is the only way to seed the soil for happiness to blossom. Listen, if someone offered you $10 million dollars to inject heroin into the arms of school children, would you do it? Of course not. It would be incongruent and whatever you bought with the $10 million dollars would be poisoned. This is what capitalism misses. The emphasis on the "bottom line" - namely ROI (Return on Investment) to shareholders - has led this system astray. We now know that watching numbers on a screen next to words such as "Net Worth," "Net Gain" and "Total" does not make people happy. Once financial security - a roof over your head and food on your plate - is attained then happiness rises very little by accumulating wealth for the sake of accumulating wealth. The status games that we play have no winners. The exclusivity of gated houses, gated communities, private jets and exclusive lounges do not correlate with happiness. F. Scott Fitzgerald supposedly once said to Ernest Hemingway, "You know, the rich are different from you and me." Hemingway replied, "Yes. They have more money." The human experience is more greatly influenced by secure connections with other people than it is by having closets full of expensive clothing. You can only wear one pair of shoes at a time. So what is the point of 1,000 pairs of shoes - especially when you know that almost half of the people on planet earth are impoverished? The widening disparity in wealth and classes in Western civilization is the result of the increasing exploitation of labor by capital. Nietzsche wrote, "Life itself is will to power." If you frame "why" people do what they do in terms of exercising power then you can even explain suicide bombers and school shootings. But here in Western civilization, most people reading or listening to this book have the privilege and luxury of choosing whether to exert power in positive or negative directions. And this is why Part 3 of this book is important: the root cause of all of our problems, in my humble opinion, is our educational system. We need to create a system that inspires future generations to choose compassion over competition. The power of "dominating" over others by attaining straight A's in school or large salaries or net worths as adults do not help most people achieve what their hearts truly crave. So now that you know that you probably became somewhat misguided by growing up in such a competitive system, and that your body's normal reaction to this system is to be wired & tired, now you can choose to create a system that is more propitious, one that has a better chance in resulting in authentic happiness rather than little power grabs. We can now see that our primacy that our educational system places on "thinking" since Descartes results in malaise. "Your best thinking got you here." So how can we think "better?" More positively? More compassionately, more harmoniously? How can we cultivate equanimity?

This is why I created a "path" - one particular path - one that I embrace but may not completely work for you. Maybe you have to cut your own path. My hope is that the tools and practices of Part 1 of this book along with subjects covered in Part 3 inspire you to try a road less traveled, like I did during those 25 years of intense seeking and what I continue to do by taking classes. What I have learned from a lifetime of education is that the only thing that correlates strongly with authentic happiness is the quality of our intimate relationships, i.e., love. And if you want to have high quality intimate relationships then you cannot be superficial or fake. When you put my proposed path to authenticity together - namely Attachment, Atonement, Attunement, Presence and Congruence - then you'll be able to show up authentically for all of your relationships and one of the by-products of those loving relationships will be happiness and the lessening of disillusionment, disenchantment, disappointment and discontentment.

Now let's discuss contemporary spirituality and see if we can re-enchant you after previously being turned off by religion(s).

When people say, "The New Age," they are usually referring to drug-addled hippies who are doing nothing productive with their lives; however, most of what is pejoratively referred to as "New Age" is Buddhism repurposed by capitalist Westerners, resulting in glib bunk. I prefer to discuss spirituality and the influence of Eastern thought on our society - primarily through practices such as yoga and meditation - but without an understanding of the paradigms out of which yoga and meditation bloomed, the practices are useless.

Following Alan Watts and many other sages, I have espoused and taught Advaita Vedanta for many years. In terms of Advaita Vedanta, everything that human beings perceive through our five senses and chunk into narratives is "maya" - illusory and ephemeral. Then there is also Brahman, the "Real" (capital 'R'), which I heard best translated as "that without attributes." Brahman is ineffable. If you can say it, or think it, then it's not it. Think of the Matrix, or everythingness, or even infinity - something literally so expansive and all-encompassing that your mind cannot comprehend it. That's why in the Judeo-Christian tradition god is written G-d: because no word can contain or describe god.

"It is only the unthinkable that is worth thinking. Who would ever want to think the thinkable?" ~ Helene Cisoux

123

Via our five senses, human beings can only consciously interact with the "real" (small 'r'); we need to transcend our consciousness - to go to the other side of cognition and the rational mind as well as language - to realize the "Real." For those trying to fathom the apparent paradox, here is the answer to your question: maya is subsumed by Brahman. Atman is the self but is usually translated into English with a capital "S" to designate "Higher Self," more closely affiliated to what we consider to be the Should. Beyond human perception and cognition, beyond the maya that we experience, Atman equals or is united or at one with Brahman. Tat tvam asi. You are 'that' (the ineffable divine). We are all really one interconnected pulsing being. And maya is subsumed by Brahman.

"And a man's life's no more than to say One." ~ Hamlet

Again, for me the problem is that the prefrontal cortex is primarily a binary machine, understanding things only by juxtaposing them with their opposites. There is a Buddhist adage that states "One mountain; many paths." The mountain is what we today call "Spirituality." As I will discuss below, meditation and yoga are like walking up the mountain, ayahuasca is like taking a helicopter to the top, and DMT is like taking a rocket ship. Over the past ten years, I have received numerous calls asking if I - as a licensed psychotherapist - recommend working with plant medicine to treat sundry traumas and/or resultant afflictions. In addition, I have seen many clients who have asked me to help them integrate what they experienced while working with plant medicine.

Firstly, in the United States of America, the primary component of Ayahuasca, DMT, is a Schedule 1 drug so it would be idiotic on many levels for a licensed psychotherapist to recommend to any clients doing something illegal. However, because of my colorful interdisciplinary academic background, I feel qualified to opine on what occurs to human consciousness and the metaphysics that allows for that alternate reality to be temporarily experienced when one ingests ayahuasca.

I recommend that anyone interested in spirituality read the 8th century Hindu sage Sankara, the Upanishads, and anything else concerning Advaita Vedanta. Even though the Hindu tradition is worlds away from South America, I believe that Eastern metaphysics, ontology and epistemology will help Westerners understand the effects of ayahuasca.

The problems with ayahuasca and DMT lie in the fact that human beings vastly over-estimate the limitations of human consciousness, what it can comprehend and what it cannot. For example, it is impossible for you to imagine infinity. You may have what Wittgenstein called a "placeholder," such as an image you once saw of the cosmos, but you cannot imagine infinity. The finite mind cannot come close to conceiving the infinite; it is constricted by arbitrary categories such as space and time. An analogy that helps to indicate this is, "It's like trying to pour the ocean into a thimble."

Again, after researching Advaita Vedanta, you will understand that everything human beings perceive through our five senses and chunk into narratives is "maya" — illusory and ephemeral. And sages have been trying for aeons to transcend human consciousness - to go to the other side of cognition and the rational mind as well as language - to "realize" (experience, or to become at one with the "Real.")

Most people are highly addicted to their senses of self. Our egos are thousands of times more arrogant than we can ever know. Our egos believe that we "know" things and this is where studying epistemology is useful. For instance, in my classes I ask if anyone knows how — HOW — gravity works. We all know the formula to calculate the effect of gravity but try to name any Western physicist who can explain what magnetic energies or waves or currencies or atoms or quarks are functioning that keep us from flying off of the earth. There is no such physicist. Causality — the mandate of science — has not been established for even the most simple of concepts that most humans accept as truth even though nobody understands exactly how it works: gravity.

Ayahuasca blows out the ego and self. DMT collapses the subject/object distinction. The subject is you; the object is whatever is "out there" and how you perceive it. This false dichotomy is best explicated by languaging: if you say, "I am experiencing the essential oneness of the universe," then obviously you are contradicting yourself because there would be no "I" to experience that. It would be more accurate to utter "oneness-ness" or "everythingness" or to just accept the fact the word ineffable means that there are no words that can describe it. Psychologically, if you study Lacan then you would agree that language actually alienates us from phenomena. Whatever you can formulate in words is not Real; words are mere symbolic representations that indicate the real as Magritte so aptly displayed in "The Treachery of Images" (i.e., you cannot smoke a painting of a pipe).

This is why soaring up the mountain is often daunting and overwhelming. Our limited language-based mind's inability to comprehend the fact that we are really all interconnected in one infinite pulsing matrix is why some people freak out on ayahuasca or have challenges integrating what they experienced when they return to their quotidian, individual, ego-based existences. R.D. Laing thought that schizophrenics had the most accurate perceptions of reality. But for a non-schizophrenic to surrender to that unchunked incomprehensibleness and unforeseeable uncertainty is usually quite terrifying at first. For as Gertrude Stein said of Oakland, "There's no there there." Our minds always seek sure footing; the ground beneath our feet shifting is quite unsettling, disturbing.

Science has reduced human beings to cells and molecules and smaller and smaller bits and parts. Thus, when a person experiences the sensation of ineffable unlimited expansiveness — an EVERYTHINGNESS not articulable by any words— it is frequently uber intense. This is why studying Advaita Vedanta is the best preparation for working with plant medicine, to help understand the inversion that maya is the hallucination and that the temporary yet timeless unfathomable everythingness that one experiences while one is self-less is the Real. You are the hallucination; the "you" is illusory; the self is a fiction. If that is too difficult for you to digest then I suggest that you stay clear of ayahuasca and DMT, because when you return to maya you will not have the tools to integrate this apparent paradox. And once you realize that the self - your self - is a fiction then you really can't do anything other than espouse relativism. You will see any dogmatism as futile power grabs and choose compassion over competition.

And this is why my concept of awakening and learning to surf paradoxes that I'll discuss in Chapter 10 is so important. I have never believed that a human can attain a permanent state of enlightenment. Anyone who claims to be enlightened is usually a sociopath. The problem, again, is that the human mind breaks things down into antinomies that are either/or rather than "and." How can you be G-d and Bob Smith the insurance salesman at the same time? How can you be the entire universe and the Google coding engineer at the same time? How can you get stressed out about traffic if you were blissfully "at one" with the Real?

So we taste the nectar of the divine through yoga, meditation, being in nature, and through plant medicine and then have to integrate that experience into our mundane, corporeal existences.

For me, after learning about spirituality I was able to tweak the narrative of my life to accept why I became who I was. After 25 years of having an adverse relationship with the scars on my face, I consciously chose what was hitherto unfathomable. "I'm supposed to have these scars on my face. I'm supposed to have permanent discomfort," I uttered. Since I'll never be able to go back in time and remove my scars, the sooner that I stop wanting

128

to change the unchangeable, the sooner I will be able to alleviate the woulda-shoulda-coulda-didn't resentments that used to keep me awake at night.

Narrative therapists help clients choose more propitious illusions. And this is what I consider to be leading an "awakened" life - to know that you are choosing the most accurate and propitious illusion possible, the one that will help engender authentic and compassionate relationships and keep you at the high end of your happiness spectrum. Atonement is tantamount to OWNING all of your history and threading it with a narrative so that you understand your triggers and compensations and why you became who you are today. Once you OWN your life you will stop the resentment-making machine - woulda-coulda-shoulda-didn't - that is actually at the root of much of your disillusionment, disenchantment and disappointment.

So in the grand scheme of reality, the crisis or rupture that you experienced that crushed your faith in the reality into which you were thrown and didn't hitherto question: the systems of our educational system, labor, capitalism, our form of democracy, working 40 hours in 5 days per week, fossil fuels, pharmaceuticals, vacations, status symbols - all of the things that most people consider to be "normal." But now you know that this "normal" does not bring with it happiness. Actually, this "normal" causes many people to be both anxious and depressed. So you are reading this book because you want to minimize depression and anxiety, you want to construct a life that will be more favorable for keeping you at the higher range of your happiness spectrum. From the Harvard longitudinal study, we know that the primary thing that correlates with happiness, the opposite of feeling wired & tired, is the quality of our intimate relationships. From the studies on Attachment Theory, we all know that most of us have fairly unrefined tools to being in intimate relationships. My proposal is that our best shot for being in secure relationships is to learn how to be authentic. To make conscious choices and to have the personal integrity to abide by those choices. To be congruent. To know why we think the shit that we think (and by 'shit' I mean our fears and prejudices, the paradigms we developed from our insecure attachment dynamics) and to lean into being vulnerable, compassionate and authentic.

Chapter 9. Retirement

Although the idea of military retirement dates back to the Romans, the practice of retirement for the general population and having a pension or funds to support your life is only around 150 years old. Max Weber in 1905 in "The Protestant Ethic and the Spirit of Capitalism" argued that Protestantism propagated capitalism with the ethos that God rewarded those who worked hard. The twentieth century in Western civilization witnessed the human lifespan practically double, mostly due to the spread of toilets and public sanitation systems combined with miraculous medical advances. People started to live longer and didn't necessarily want to spend those extra years working, although human beings tend to tire of being oppressed and exploited or jump through hoops like dancing bears irrespective of how much money they are being paid. In fact, most people probably viewed retirement as a reward for 45 years of steady labor. In 1935 Franklin Roosevelt managed to pass the Social Security Act which provided financing for people over 65 to stop working. As you probably know, the average lifespan at that time was 62 years-old; hence most people at that time did not benefit from this act.

Currently I am unaware of any courses in our educational system on "How To Live A Long Life" or "What To Do When You Retire." I have mixed feelings on the concept of retirement. Wouldn't it be better to be retired when you were young and potent, say in your twenties, than when you were old and haggard, lugging your decrepit body from cruise ship buffet line to guided bus tour of some semi-exotic locale? In my case, I spent all of my

disposable income on my education so I will never be able to retire unless I win the lottery, which will be extremely difficult, seeing as I don't ever play it. But I enjoyed maybe a little too much
freedom during my prime earning years and really never expected to live very long so I am lucky to earn my living doing
what I love… helping others, teaching, and writing; thus, I would
be in no rush to retire anyhow.

But for those who were not independent contractors and
punched a clock for 40 or 45 years, I imagine that retirement
sounds like just rewards for working hard. Moving to a retirement community in clement weather (Florida) makes me think
of Sartre's famous phrase from "No Exit:" "L'enfer, c'est les autres" (Hell is other people); however, I have recently read of the
rapid spread of sexually transmitted diseases in many of the mega
communities so I will assume proximity to hundreds of thousands of age-appropriate partners - like in college - has its ad-
vantages for finding partners for golf, tennis and other activities.

What would a course in "How To Retire" instruct? I imagine
that for most people retirement is not a surprise unless it is a sudden forced retirement. In an odd way our culture is very agist.
George Bernard Shaw said, "Youth is wasted on the young" and
it does seem as if there are infinitely more opportunities for
young idealistic 20-somethings to get into trouble than for 70-
somethings. If one has had children and those children have had
children then most of your joy will come from being a grandpar-
ent - not having the responsibilities of disciplining these young
people but reaping the rewards of being positive influences in

their lives. But if grandchildren don't take up much of your retirement years, then what should one do?

This is the time to engage in the life of the mind - go to museums, symphonies, plays, attend lectures, take classes. At UCLA
the Senior Scholar program allows any residents of Los Angeles
over 50 years old to audit any classes. Dr. Terry Small found it
helped people live longer to be intellectually stimulated so he created the Senior Scholar program and I have been attending classes at UCLA as well as concerts and lectures and gatherings.
There happen to be colleges and universities all across America
so if you're retired and are looking for ways to be stimulated intellectually, I would suggest starting by researching ways to get
involved in your local colleges. And if you enjoy the energy of
young people, once you retire you will have plenty of time to vol-
unteer to teach these young people some of the things that you
learned while visiting planet earth during the time many years
ago since you were their age. There are all sorts of programs at
libraries and schools for retired people to mentor young people,
teach them how to read or do math… the opportunities abound!

For me the giant rabbit hole is consciousness, the mind, so I
have always been fascinated by what artists, writers, musicians,
and philosophers are thinking when they create their artworks. I
try to understand what they are trying to express and how their
mental lives are similar and different from my own. Most of my
free time is spent exploring art and music and I would suggest
that newly retired people make conscious decisions to remain curious and stimulated rather than get distracted by purely leisure
and entertainment activities.

And, of course, as your life winds down and more and more of your friends, family members and loved ones take their leave, you will probably want to spend much time navel-gazing and wondering if you lived a good life, if you could you have done things differently (No, you could not have), what would have happened if you had made other decisions, etc. Personally I was struck by Atul Gawande's book "Being Mortal" for his astute observation that death is almost hidden from people in Western civilization - we don't sit around with corpses for days nor are most "meat" items in our supermarkets recognizable as an animal that was once breathing and eating and pooping while locked inside its pen or cage. Hence we are often surprised when mortality appears.

A brief note about the end of life:

I used to get peeved when I called Federal Express and their voice answering system said, "Please hold. A representative will be with you momentarily." I thought, "Well, that won't do much good. I won't be able to say everything I have to say during just one moment. The primary definition of "momentarily" is during one moment, not in one moment. Thus, when I write the words "you will die momentarily" I mean that your transition from life to death will occur rapidly, not imminently. The dying process may or may not take a long time (actually it already started the moment you were born), but the transition from life to death occurs in a single moment, suddenly, momentarily. How often should one think about his or her upcoming rendezvous with non-existence? As will be discussed in Part 3, Heidegger famously called us "Beings unto death."

Our perception of time is curious. Ponder this:

Fact: You didn't exist for millions of years.

Fact: You were born and your body will inhabit a minuscule spot-on planet earth for a finite period of time.

Fact: You will die and no longer exist for millions of years again.

Thus, in relation to the time you spend not being alive, your life is obviously precious. Thinking on this grand scale makes every day a gift, something to be cherished. Right?

We all know that living life is fatal. And yet so many human beings — particularly teenagers and drug addicts — seem to live their lives as if they were invincible.

Why do so many human beings believe that hoarding material possessions will somehow stave off their future non-existence? Secret: It won't. "You can't take it with you."

Why do so many human beings believe that leaving a legacy will make them feel better about their fleeting existence? Secret: You don't worry about what other people think of you when you're dead. Why do so many human beings believe that filling up their lives with distractions will engender lasting happiness? I guess the best way to sum up my question is how often should one think about his or her upcoming rendezvous with non-existence? I am uncertain of the proper dosage of death needed to appreciate life. This is one of the many blessings/curses of human consciousness. My cat, Helen - to the best of my knowledge - has no inkling of non-existence. She does her best to avoid pain, keep her belly sated, play when feeling playful, and get a decent amount of rest, but she appears to have no existential issues whatsoever. It is only human consciousness that provides such intense biases.

In my humble opinion, there are two main problems with death:

1. Consciousness fallaciously informs us that we would miss things. "Shit! I can't die now! I haven't climbed Mount Everest yet!" This is one of those "Half empty/Half full" scenarios. Yes, there are obviously infinite phenomena that you will miss. Duh. But why not focus on the wonderful things you did experience instead of the things you imagine you woulda-coulda-shoulda-didn't experience? Even dour Wittgenstein's last words were, "Tell them it was a wonderful life."

2. Although being dead is painless, the dying part of the process is often quite painful. Sometimes it's even a bloody mess. Sometimes it appears to be interminable. For the human body is a wildly resilient machine — just ask any of the millions of people who fail at killing themselves every year.

However... however... almost dying — almost as in horseshoes and hand grenades but not in pregnancy or running a marathon — is usually quite a consciousness-raising event. It immediately takes one off of autopilot and allows appreciation of our short time on earth to be in the forefront of consciousness; a near-death experience is the one transformational incident that can arouse or goad one into replacing resentment with gratitude. Rick Hanson taught me that "You can't pull all of the weeds in the garden. But you can plant flowers." You can't weed out all of your woulda-coulda-shoulda-didn't resentments but you can plant little flowers of gratitude. And if you tend to your mental garden every day, there's no telling what beautiful little thing might sprout.

Human consciousness is a rough beast. It causes us to categorize phenomena as black or white, a particle or a wave, good and bad, good and evil. It causes ideology which causes prejudice which causes dogmatism which causes war. The thought "Nobody gets out of life alive" levels the playing field, makes ideology seem absurd, prejudice seem ignorant, dogmatism seem idiotic, and war seem insane. The thought "Nobody gets out of life alive" foments compassion. And it will all be over sooner than you ever imagined. The final moment will be extremely sudden.

We are the only animals who know that we are going to die and that knowledge affects how we live, how we choose to live. Nietzsche famously wrote, "Some are born posthumously" meaning that he was resigned to a painful life of almost daily suffering because he knew that he was creating a body of work that would exist after he died. For my generation and thereafter, I think many of us identify more closely with the phrase "Instant gratification takes too long." Most of us can only think about our next meal or vacation, not 50 years after we are dead.

I watched a dear friend prepare for death after the doctor informed him that his third bout with liver cancer had no remedy. It is a gruesome process and most of us want to exit with a little more dignity with which we entered, which might not be possible. I watched my 97-year-old grandmother end up in a fetal position wearing diapers, just as she had done 96 1/2 years ago. Full

137

circle. But how do we prepare for this? I think the best solace is knowing that you lived life to your fullest capacity when you had the chance. That you OWNED all of your experiences and BECAME WHO YOU WERE SUPPOSED TO BE. That you had personal integrity and were able to make amends when you lacked integrity. That you loved with abandon and tried to be a positive influence on everyone's life that you touched.

Nobody on their deathbed ever said, "I should have spent more time at the office" or "I would have been happy if I had earned more zeros on my Bitcoin investment." Most people, to the best of my understanding, say something to the effect of "I should have loved more." Love is really the only thing that counts and yet 99% of our conversations are about shopping victories, status symbols, vacation destinations, distractions, comparing ourselves with others, investments, dysfunctional relationships, food, sports and games. We invest so much time in things that ultimately don't matter. Life is short. Don't waste any remaining time that you have left.

PART 3

Everything People Should Have Studied to Prepare Them For Adulthood

(Good news! It's not too late)

Chapter 10. Western Civilization's Greatest Hits

"I could be bounded in a nutshell and count myself a king of infinite space…" ~ Hamlet

The goal of liberal arts colleges and universities, from my perspective as a 56-year-old white male who grew up in the suburbs and graduated from 4 different universities (2 public, 2 private), should be to widen students' horizons, provide them with more choices and opportunities. Life is analogous to a tree and the more you know and experience, then the more the tree will bloom, blossom and prosper.

There is what I refer to as a "Conversation" that artists and musicians and writers as well as physicists and engineers have been engaged in for centuries in Western civilization and this "Conversation" contains hints and glimmers regarding how other humans have dealt with similar existential issues - such as the phenomenon referred to in this book as "wired & tired." Provocative paintings and jazz explorations as well as theoretical experiments and thirty-page advanced math equations about space create ruptures in extant consciousness and spin the ethos in a new direction. Think of the advent of rap music and hip-hop or cubist paintings… all of these events as well as discussions of them in newspapers and journals are what I call "The Conversation." This evolution of Western civilization and the analysis of segues and inspirations has always been very exciting to me and my hope is that it is equally exciting to you. I love learning new things and seeing things from new perspectives. **The fun and irreverent glossing over of the liberal arts in this chapter is meant to help you discover new ways of understanding the evolution of our society that will revitalize your life and give you a greater purpose.**

Being able to be part of this conversation about the essences and trajectory of our culture is one of the main purposes of college in my humble opinion. In particular, knowledge of the major themes and players in the liberal arts will help you later in life know that you are not alone in whatever you are feeling and/or exploring intellectually. I believe that art and philosophy and psychology and all of the other disciplines are part of one larger "Conversation" and that we have to know the past in order to change and hopefully improve it.

When I teach workshops, I tell the class, "If you told my grandmother in 1972 that someday a black man would be president, gay people could marry, marijuana would be legal, and there would be transgender bathrooms," she would have looked at you askew. Imagine how people in the year 2100 will look back on us. They might say, "Oh those morons, they had to use mobile phones - they didn't realize they could communicate telepathically." Or, "Oh those morons, they had to use airplanes - they didn't realize they could teleport themselves." Nobody who can read these words was raised in a vacuum; we were all "thrown" into language and sets of mores, ethics, and propriety. My hope is that my cursory overview inspires 18-22 year-olds to take classes they may not have taken in college, and to inspire those over 22 to take online classes or benefit from the thousands and thousands of hours of psychology, philosophy, and sociology explications that abound on YouTube and other media.

The ultimate intention of widening horizons is to have you release the clinging you have to YOUR version of reality, to allow for possibilities of infinite perspectives. If you already are familiar with the adage "The map is not the territory" then you may want to skip ahead to the conclusions. Prejudices, I believe, are built from ignorance. I could be wrong, but I believe that the more knowledgeable one is, the more likely they are to be relativistic ("live and let live") rather than dogmatic ("there's my way and the wrong way").

I used to joke that the primary things students learn at university in America are fucking and drinking, usually (unfortunately) learning the former due to the latter. Our society was previously very puritanical and oppressive; thus, when younger adults are released into the wild for the first time in their lives and live away from their parents, many of them abuse their new freedoms and party quite intensely.

I graduated from the University of Pennsylvania in 1988 and looking back we can see that the 80s were a culmination of the "greed is good" highly competitive "winner-takes-all" society. Cocaine was involved also. The role of university for many of my peers at that time had already diverged from its original intentions - Benjamin Franklin's ideas of the goals of education as he delineated them in the 1750. College life in the past thirty or forty years has become even more career-focused than it was in

1980s, teaching students specific knowledge so that they can maximize their earning potential over their lifespans (and pay back their student loans).

Before we get started, please allow this brief diatribe regarding how our university system has become corrupted: according to Malcolm Harris in "Kids These Days," universities used to be primarily run by professors and most teaching professors were tenured for life, obtaining 100% job security and a livable wage to freely pursue intellectual endeavors. But over the last 40 years even though most universities are still considered 501c3 non-profit corporations, they are run by MBA graduates whose goal is to maximize profits (without paying any taxes). A non-profit institution designed to maximize profits. Here is a list of endowments of some of these fine institutions of higher learning in billions:

Harvard University	$40.58
Yale University	$31.20
Stanford University	$28.90
Princeton University	$26.56
University of Pennsylvania	$20.50

With businesspeople instead of older professors running these universities the primacy is no longer placed on tenuring professors to bring intellectual grandeur but on Club Med type cafes, pools, stadiums and luxury dormitories. And whereas universities are free in Europe, the average American student leaves hampered with $32,731 of student debt, which comes out to hundreds of dollars per month for many years starting as soon as the students graduate. Statistically, college graduates still earn more over their lifespans than non-college graduates. Yet, many young people and middle-class families wonder if the extraordinarily high tuitions are worth the investment.

With this type of burden it is no wonder that students are more focused on taking classes that will prepare them for high paying jobs (to pay off their student loans faster) rather than becoming well-rounded human beings. As opposed to students being forced to take classes as part of a core curriculum in subjects that they will never use, I believe that the following liberal arts subjects are the ones that will help prepare them for the ups and downs of adult life - the ruptures that cause existential questions - even if studying these subjects does not immediately translate into helping to allay the crushing burdens of student debt: psychology, philosophy, literature, history, anthropology, art history, and sociology, as well as overviews of political science and economics to help understand how the world is transforming.

In my classes I joke quite often that my mind makes fortune cookies. For instance, from the thousands of pages of Upanishads I conclude "Atman equals Brahman;" from the Bhagavad Gita I conclude "Follow your dharma." Thus, my overviews of the disciplines that follow are really just my highly reductionistic opinions regarding the salient features that would help students waylay crises and adults being wired & tired 25 years down the road. For older adults I hope that my mere mentioning of some of these disciplines and thinkers inspires them to revitalize their intellectual lives.

Irrespective of what you actually studied at university, **in this chapter I am going to lay down the foundations that I believe you should have covered in order to stave off future crises or ruptures. In addition, I am going to irreverently lead you to my personal conclusions of what is important about studying these particular disciplines and subjects.** Hint: in the end, through my irreverence, I hope to make a case for relativism à la French post-structuralism, in contrast to the dogmatism that leads to fundamentalism that leads to terrorism and war. Subtly, through this extremely brief intellectual overview of Western civilization I aspire to tease you into believing that the solution to what most of what ails us hails from the East: namely compassion, à la His Holiness the Dalai Lama, is our best bet for both survival and happiness.

Academics will turn over in their untenured chairs at how I have brazenly reduced thousands, if not millions, of pages and scores of years of their peers' *oeuvres* to ditties the size of fortune cookie adages. These gross generalizations will easily allow me to be granted the pejorative moniker of "dilettante." I do not deny it. Again, the point of this chapter is to glean not the actual theories of the below theoreticians but to have a 40,000-foot overview of the past few hundreds of years in Western civilization so that readers understand that everything they think and read and do is CONTINGENT and RELATIVE, and that there are myriad other things that they could just as well think and read and do.

Very quickly I will arrive at a place in the philosophy section deconstructing our notion of "truth." The fundamentalists setting other people on fire, chopping off their heads, crazy-gluing their rectums and throwing them off of buildings believe in a "truth." Those who disagree with their "truth" are considered "infidels" and the only good infidel is a tortured and murdered infidel according to some fundamentalists. These fundamentalists could also be referred to as dogmatists. People who are dogmatic believe that their "truth" is a one-size-fits-all proposition and that they possess it and must force all others to believe what they believe. The antinomy to keep in mind here is dogmatism vs. relativism. Relativists believe that everyone is free to believe what they want to believe (as long as it causes no harm to others). Dogmatists try to reify their own beliefs by inflicting them on others. Relativists believe that "truth" is relative to cultures, places, and languages and that the world would be a better place if all of the tribes and countries allowed the other tribes and countries to live in peace rather than proselytize and attempt to inflict their "truths" upon them. So I am not an academic who is going to lecture you on psychology, philosophy, etc. I am a disrupter that hopes to inspire you to think for yourself and possibly lure you towards the opinion that the finest utterance about this bizarre concept of "truth" was made by Nietzsche when he said, "We have art lest we perish of the truth." Following this deconstruction, the only overall logical way of interacting is through compassion, empathy, and compersion, not through the competition that we learned in our educational system.

146

Psychology

Seeing as a plethora of adults in our society are suffering from numerous mental health issues that fall under the rubric of "Psychology," I believe that all college students should know a brief history of psychology in Western civilization, at least psychology beginning with Sigmund Freud who knew he was setting our society into a new orbit when he published "The Interpretation of Dreams" in 1900.

Firstly, a gander at the current Diagnostic and Statistical Manual of Disorders (known colloquially as the DSM) should reveal that there is really no good definition of mental wellness. A more scrupulous reading will uncover that "labor" is really the only consistent barometer of whether or not an individual is well. Is he or she a "productive" member of society? And if you are not a "productive" member of society then the pharmaceutical industry certainly has some medications that will enable you to sit at your desk or stand in your position at a factory for eight hours per day five days per week fifty weeks per year. (By the way, have you ever wondered how old is our notion of a 40-hour work week? Was it better or worse before then?)

The bandwidth of human emotions necessary to be a productive laborer is extremely constricted. Most excessively angry or sad people find it difficult to focus on any job for a week. Or maybe even a day. Or maybe an hour. So people who suffer from depressed moods - more than twenty million of them every day in our society - are provided with medications so that they can perform whatever tasks they are being paid to perform. In general, bosses and co-workers find workers who are crying or yelling

147

to be disruptive to the workflow and try to remedy these heightened emotions as soon as possible. But what if it is the actual (mind-numbing, soul-sucking) job that is causing the depression? Or what if the boss is assigning one-hundred hours of work for a supposed forty-hour work week and the people at the surrounding desks or positions are not complaining? And - like at Amazon - you know that the 10% least productive people will be fired at the end of the year? Wouldn't that cause constant anxiety?

So psychology classes should offer a 40,000-foot overview of mental wellness in our society and discover why so many people are unwell. Here's a brief history:

Sigmund Freud (1856-1939) was trained as a medical doctor and claimed that he "discovered" the human unconscious. Victorian England and Christianity had repressed human sexuality and Freud thought that many of the afflictions that ailed Europeans were the result of this repressed sexuality. The unconscious did not care much for all of the previously mentioned denial of natural urges and revolted in myriad ways: dreams could be interpreted in light of this new paradigm, hysterical women could be cured by vaginal massage as Freud learned from his teacher Charcot, and a "talking cure" known as psychoanalysis could uncover and then somehow mitigate many afflictions, according to Doctor Freud, through an "aha" moment where the doctor led the patient to remember a violation of her psyche and/or body that occurred many moons ago. The main concepts, most of which Freud created as tools and many of which were mistranslated into English, are Id, Ego, Superego, libido, Oedipus complex and repression.

Freud had a few disciples who all branched off and created interesting theories. Thanks to the work of Joseph Campbell I would argue that Carl Jung is currently both the most prominent and interesting of Freud's disciples. However, it is very easy to see why Freud and Jung split: Freud remained steadfast in his belief of psychology as scientific and Jung became more interested in stories, narratives, and cross-cultural archetypes that shaped those stories.

Jung searched far and wide across mythologies and found similarities thus proposing common archetypes that were alive and distributed through what he called "the collective unconscious." The possibility that common threads of not only stories but personality types are wafting through the ethers that circumnavigate our cosmos is not scientifically provable. Thus, Jung's theories would seem like twaddle to a chemist or biologist or engineer. And yet, I have met extremely erudite and fascinating people who have studied his work for 50 or 60 years. Personally, I credit Jung with cracking open the door to narrative therapy and untethering psychology from "science" while also (following Schopenhauer) introducing yoga, kundalini energy and concepts such as synchronicity to Western civilization.

Other psychologists like Pavlov starting in the 1920s moved towards trying to explain behaviors scientifically and then numerous theorists started to move towards studying cognition and consciousness. In the 1930s Piaget in particular theorized about the evolution of how babies learn and traced developmental phases in infants.

In the 1940s Carl Rogers developed "client-centered therapy" in which therapists created safe spaces with positive regard for clients so that they could "re-parent" themselves. This is the type of psychotherapy that I espouse and advocate - especially for people who are wired & tired. Paying someone to validate our emotional experiences, given all of the pressures and stresses of modern life, is well worth the time and money.

Starting in the 1950s the first Diagnostic and Statistical Manual of Mental Disorders was published and it listed all of the psychological problems as delineated by the American Psychiatric Association. Basically, everything that was not conducive to an individual being a productive member of the labor force was pathologized. Also, you should note that until 1973 homosexuality was considered to be a medical disorder so I'm sure you'll agree that the DSM is dynamic and that certain people - like those involved in Big Pharma - have a vested interest in pathologizing many phenomena.

Upon further inspection I believe that one main takeaway from the DSM is that psychiatric problems can be divided into two main categories: cognitive and emotional (mood). Cognitive issues such as schizophrenia mean that the person's cognition does not operate in the way we universally accept cognition to operate in Western civilization. These people suffer from visual and auditory hallucinations, delusions - sights and sounds that only they can see and hear. The other set of issues are characterized as mood disorders and today primarily include depression and anxiety; most people today refer to anyone who suffers from extreme moods as "bipolar." The exact definitions of bipolar 1 and bipolar 2 include intense manic episodes interspersed with debilitating depressive episodes but nonetheless these are *mood disorders*; hallucinations, delusions, and hearing voices are *cognitive disorders*.

Science is created by trial-and-error processes; we all know that Viagra began as a heart medication. Similarly, certain pharmaceuticals affect the ways our brains function and are used to "correct" cognitive distortions or stymie intense mood swings. Just to play devil's advocate, allow me to mention that British psychiatrist R.D. Laing believed that schizophrenics have the purist relationship with "reality" (what is "out there," not inside of our noggins) and that human consciousness chunks what is amorphously "out there" into categories such as space (distance, color, height, weight, objects, parts, phenomena) and time (past, present, future).

Regarding the seemingly infinite ailments defined by the DSM, there are psychotherapists such as me who follow theories by psychologists such as Rollo May and Thomas Szasz who believe that many of the putative "disorders" are either completely fabricated or are trauma-based. That if the subject grew up on a desert island in an idyllic setting with continuously loving caregivers that these supposed emotional disorders would never arise.

For example, when working with clients who suffer from Obsessive Compulsive Disorder, I often say, "The symptoms of your OCD began as a SOLUTION to a problem. We agree that there is no gene that causes people to check their stoves or the locks on their doors hundreds of times before leaving the house — correct? OCD is not something that anyone is born with - correct? There is not a gene that causes compulsion - correct? It is a reaction. It is your younger mind's best shot at solving a traumatic problem.

For me - someone who suffers from OCD - the narrative that I have constructed along with the assistance of psychotherapists is as follows: I was 18 years-old. A hole had been drilled through the top of my tibia to pull my knee down from my hip and straighten out my mangled leg using a 40-pound pulley. (For those who managed to escape anatomy class, the tibia is the large bone below the knee inside of the leg; it is located under the skin and cartilage so you can imagine the amount of spurting blood caused by a power drill going in one side of a leg, through the bone, and out the other side.) Besides being in agonizing pain from multiple fractures, I had to suffer the humiliation of not being able to get out of traction and the hospital bed to go to a bathroom. I was not in control. My cleanliness and safety depended 100% on a series of people dress in white coats at the end of red button to bring me bed pans. I believe that my mind said, "This is awful. I am not in control. I do not have autonomy. I do not have agency. I am 18 years-old and dependent on other adult humans to help me perform basic bodily functions. This is humiliating. There's no privacy. I am never going to let this happen again." Later I began to notice symptoms diagnosable as OCD: repeatedly checking door locks, adamantly believing I left the stove on, overzealously cleaning, highly intense organization and labeling of files, paying all bills as soon as they were received and well in advance (830/850 credit score — yippee!) etc. in general, being a control freak (in your humble opinion) and having an obsession with fierce independence yet not even trusting my own ability to maintain order. Somewhat and regularly discombobulating. Frantic. Frenetic.

152

From all of my academic studies over the past 38 years I feel confident in stating that the past does not exist, no longer exists. There may be photos, memories, videos, audio recordings, sketches, but that week 38 years ago when I was physically incapacitated has not existed for a long time. In fact, recently I attended a boxing class, a swimming class, a yoga class - none of which would be possible for someone immobile in a hospital bed. And yet, the defense mechanisms that my mind created to try to stave off another incapacitating situation incapacitated me in sundry ways for many years. Or at least pissed off many friends who had to wait in the street while I checked my stove and front door lock again and again. (On the other hand, my landlord in Paris didn't seem terribly dismayed when I paid my rent two years in advance.). When clients come into my office complaining about similar compulsive behaviors or obsessive thoughts, I ask them to assume a meditative posture and then we gently walk their minds backwards until they find when these "solutions" first appeared.

Then we discuss what was going in the patient's life at that time and find anything that a young mind might find traumatic — parents' divorce, a betrayal, an abandonment, a fall, the death of a loved one, a supposed failure, a humiliation, a car accident, a loss — and discuss all of the feelings around the event. We temporarily construct a narrative (all narratives are dynamic, constantly in flux — you and your mind recount stories about the same incident differently over time) about the origin of the obsessive thoughts and compulsive behaviors. Then I ask a series of absurd, rhetorical questions unequivocally proving that the event and subsequent trauma are long gone and the younger mind's "solutions" are now trying to solve a problem that no longer exists. Finally we create a phrase or mantra that the patient employs whenever the thoughts or behaviors rear their loving heads. Because at some point in time, these thoughts and behaviors were our young mind's solution to a problem.

OK, so that's one example of a different perspective on what the DSM delineates as Obsessive Compulsive Disorder. Personally, I believe that **many of our adult behaviors - including what we commonly refer to as afflictions and addictions - began as reactions or compensations to traumas.** Having an understanding of psychology would help people recognize their own reactions and compensations and help prevent those compensations from into transmuting into debilitating afflictions.

Please forgive that brief digression into the DSM and my own experience with OCD but I believe it is important to understand the system of thought that governs our mental health industry as well as some of the other ways of viewing what our society considers to be mental disorders. Let us move forwards into the 1950s following the two world wars, millions of young men dying on the battlefield, millions of people exterminated like animals in concentration camps, millions of people burned or exploded to death from bombings, and the constant fear of Russia launching a nuclear attack on the United States. The 1950s saw the birth of humanistic psychology and in 1958 Harry Harlow published "The Nature of Love," which described the importance of attachment and love in rhesus monkeys.

The 1960s saw an explosion of various movements and myriad influences and explorations. So many brilliant theorists dove

154

deep into their own minds and used sundry resources to research the nooks and crannies of the human brain as it developed in the post World Wars, nuclear family, American Dream (house and washing machine) society. My particular interest, obviously stemming from my own childhood and highly critical, emotionally withholding parents (although their memories of my childhood differ wildly from my own), is Attachment Theory. In the 1960s British psychologist John Bowlby noticed that babies became distressed when their mothers were absent. Go figure. A few years later his colleague Mary Ainsworth developed an experiment called "The Strange Situation" where mothers left their babies in a strange room for a brief period and then returned. From these experiments Ainsworth theorized that people develop either secure or insecure attachment styles very early in life. A third of the babies somehow knew that their mothers would not put them in harm's way and remained calm in the strange situation, then reattached securely when their mothers returned to the room.

However however however... two-thirds of the babies were agitated by being left alone in a strange situation and then one of two things (originally) occurred when their mothers reappeared:

1. The baby remained anxious and the mother had difficultly consoling it
2. The baby, which had probably "cried itself out" was INDIFFERENT to the mother and did not wish to reattach because it feared that this painful abandonment would recur and thus cause pain all over again. This is also known as "avoidant."

Later a third type of insecure attachment style was characterized as "disorganized" where the baby acted in extremes, first clinging desperately to the mother then pushing her away.

Personally, I believe that 1. a study of Internet dating in particular and divorce rates in general would prove that most adults today suffer from a primal abandonment wound and are fearful of connecting - also known as "avoidant"; 2. the extreme cases - those babies who displayed disorganized attachment - grew up with something that resembles what we refer to as Borderline Personality Disorder. For me, Borderline Personality Disorder, like Suicidal Ideation, is akin to terrorism: the subject does not feel heard and thus feels compelled to behave extremely, i.e., scream, threaten, leave a dead animal in your soup pot, etc. I propose that dear few people who had secure attachments with their primary caregivers for the first four years of their lives grew up to suffer from Borderline Personality Disorder. It's a silly diagnosis and most of the clients I have treated who supposedly suffer from this pathology are quite intelligent; when you maintain rigid boundaries with them and display that their terrorism is ineffectual, they choose to make healthier long-term decisions that bode better for healthy relationships (or they leave a dead rabbit in your soup pot). Essentially, they learned bad tools as children in order to get their caregivers' attention - breaking things, hysterical crying, rancid manipulation, leaving a dead animal in your refrigerator, etc. - and when provided a new set of tools they can make healthier choices.

Still regarding Attachment Theory, it is essential to be cognizant of the dynamics that we have with each of our parents because those manifest later in our adult relationships as attachment styles. For example, if our fathers or mothers were aloof and emotionally withholding, we should not be surprised if we are attracted to partners who turn out to be aloof and withholding. There is a part of us that becomes what we loved and admired as children, and there is a part of us that becomes what we hated and despised as children. Or as I state in my classes, "We become what we love (in our parents) and we become what we hate (in our parents) and BOTH are inauthentic." I believe that many adults remain conflicted because they have opposed subconscious desires: to gain the approval of their caregivers (even if they are long gone) and to individuate. Unfortunately, our basic form of individuation is to rebel, bite the nipple, define ourselves by "not" being our parents or what is referred to as "The Terrible Twos" when two year-olds continuously say "No!" to basically whatever their parents say.

But could even this be a reaction? Psychologist Arthur Janov proposed that when a parent first puts a baby down (double-entendre - here it is meant "put down to sleep," not "put down" as in one euthanizes a pet) the baby thinks "YOU'RE KILLING ME!" Subconsciously the baby knows it cannot survive alone and even though the parent explains that they will return, the baby doesn't understand language and fears death. This is the "Primal Abandonment Wound" that I believe many of my peers suffer from. It registers as a cosmic BETRAYAL. And I have found in my 16 years of practice as a psychotherapist that many clients' core wounds revolve around BETRAYAL and ABANDONMENT.

Specifically, I have found that the wounded child in all of us feels betrayed because all he or she wanted was to be loved UN-CONDITIONALLY and grew up in a society that primarily provided tools that enable us to gain love CONDITIONALLY - because we learned how to eat with a fork, use a toilet, received good grades, behaved correctly, looked good, were good athletes, spoke well, earned money, were talented, etc. This creates much resentment because even as children felt as if we were constantly "seducing" people into liking us. However the tools we learned to seduce people into liking us often are not the right tools for procuring the type of love that our hearts really yearn for later in life - they are more apt for procuring admiration. Let me ask you: would you rather be admired or loved? I am sure boatloads of people admire you but if you were laid up in the hospital for a week how many of those admirers would take time out of their busy schedules to visit you in-person and empathize with you?

Here is the conundrum: in an effort to individuate, sometimes we affiliate ourselves with people who are the exact opposite of one of our parents. Rebellion is an essential part of the individuation process - but it can also be inauthentic if it is only moving away from something rather than also moving towards something.

I believe that babies individuate the first time they recognize themselves in a mirror (as a coherent "self" distinct from their mothers), then again when they go to pre-school or school for the first time but are still living in their parents' homes; then again when if they go off to college away from home but have their parents still paying to support them; then again when they live away from their parents and learn how to support themselves as adults. There is a tension between having to obey and depend on your parents and wanting to be your own person. Note the spate of young people in the last 35-40 years who got tattoos early in life; this is a subconscious declaration, "I own my body and nobody can tell me what to do with it anymore (even if you're still paying my rent)."

We are living in fascinatingly complex and often confusing times regarding gender roles, the ways we expect men and women to act. We all agree that women should be paid equal salaries as men, yet many women still think that men should pay for meals as subconscious symbols of being providers and protectors. There is a tension between wanting to be independent and wanting to be taken care of.

One way to heal the wounds of perceived betrayal and abandonment which register in our minds as "not good enough," is through conscious loving and authentic communications. This is when we are mindfully aware of our wounds and how we learned to compensate for them as children. Usually there is some level of inauthenticity regarding these "assets." We must be aware of how we learned to seduce people into liking our "false selves" or personas and be brave enough to be authentic and vulnerable (which can be quite scary). And the first thing you need is a loving non-judgmental relationship with someone who is empathetic and who accepts the whole you, warts and all, not just the glitzy exteriors that we tend to choose to show the world - particularly the way we present our lives on the Internet.

The main take-away of learning a brief overview of the trajectory of psychology in Western civilization over the past

125 years would be to understand that dear few people who grew up on a desert island and had all of their emotional and physical needs met by their extended family or tribe would be wired & tired, would suffer from the depression and anxiety that is rampaging through Western civilization, which is built on a fictitious "winner-takes-all" highly competitive consumer-based capitalistic system where "enough is never enough." Most of the 900 pages of "disorders" of the DSM exist only in Western civilization BECAUSE THEY ARE CAUSED BY THE SUBCONSCIOUS RAMIFICATIONS OF GROWING UP AND BEING TAUGHT TO BUY A HOUSE, GO INTO DEBT, ACCRUE MATERIAL POSSESSIONS, ATTAIN USELESS STATUS SYMBOLS, BE HIP AND COOL LIKE THE PEOPLE IN THE MEDIA...

Also, because intimate relationships are the only thing that correlate strongly with happiness, as an adult, you are responsible for becoming aware of your Core Wound, your defense mechanisms, whose voice is the origin of your Inner Critic, what compensations you made for any and all of the traumas that you endured, and what set of tools you now possess to combat the bouts of depression and anxiety that are commonplace in our highly competitive, "winner-takes-all" consumer-based capitalistic system.

Regarding addiction... addiction is an extremely serious problem in our society. I feel as if once an addiction has taken root our best chance to get rid of it is to replace it with a healthier addiction. So many junkies have become yoga practitioners then yoga teachers. The 12-step program is the best game in town for alcoholics, but its success rate is still less than desirable. Diving into spirituality and focusing our energies on meditation and yoga are my best answers for clients who are looking to break addictions.

Philosophy

After taking some basic psychology classes, all college students should be required to take at least one general philosophy class - again - to know that there exists a lineage of thinkers in our culture who have been entertaining particular concepts that seem to plague people during various crises later in life.

I was taught many years ago that concepts are produced by philosophers and then eventually permute throughout the other arts and sciences. As an extreme analog, think of Leonardo da Vinci in 1489 designing the aerial screw, which is a precursor to the modern helicopter. The importance is to note shifts or ruptures that sideswipe "The Conversation" known as Western civilization onto a new, hitherto unforeseen path - like humans being able to fly like birds, a major shift in the history of humanity. French philosopher Alain Badiou calls these twists or ruptures "events" but for our purposes I am going to eventually argue that the tires started to come off the chassis of the human ideas of "truth" and "scientific knowledge" in the early 1900s - that both phenomenology and physics (Schrodinger's Cat) started to question many of the ideas we consider to be "normal;" thereafter we end up looking at sociologists and entities such as "The Frankfurt School" as well as artists to help us gain some insights into what John Stuart Mill called "Homo Economicus." In the 1880s Nietzsche wrote that our faith in a Christian god to provide "the good life" would become a faith in science; one-hundred years later I think most would agree that our faith in science morphed into a faith in money to provide "the good life." However, faith in the almighty dollar as well as other fungible and non-fungible currencies is waning and now we are amidst another rupture. But before we can understand our own psychologies and personal crises as adults, we will benefit from a rapid overview of how the other arts and sciences evolved in our culture over the most recent epochs known as modernity and post-modernity.

In this section tracing primarily through Continental Philosophy (the continent being Europe), I will argue that many of the questions philosophers raise can be viewed as theoretical gameplaying and far-fetched theorizing: sometimes - as in science fiction films and novels - these fantasies or "what if..." propositions are extremely influential and sometimes they are horribly misguided.

The word "philosophy" means "love of wisdom" but it makes sense to know philosophy is usually chunked into sub-disciplines. In no particular order, specifically the subjects that are usually studied by philosophers are as follows:

Epistemology is the study of knowledge; why and how we know the things that we think that we "know."

Metaphysics - "meta" means "beyond" is the study of things that transcend the physical (can't be weighed on a scale or viewed in a microscope) yet somehow seem to apply to all human beings.

Ontology is the study of the essential nature of reality.

Aesthetics is the study of art and the beautiful.

Existentialism is the study of why we exist.

Ethics studies what is considered right and wrong.

Logic studies how conclusions follow from certain premises.

Philosophy of Mind studies consciousness, everything that is mental, why and how we think what we think. Many laypeople conflate mind and brain and yet the relationship between the two is uncertain at best. Neurologists study the brain; philosophers study the mind. I use the following analogy: the brain is the hardware and the mind is the software or operating system.

In some ways we can see that many of the above cited subdisciplines blend into each other even though different philosophers concentrate on particular aspects. What will be important to note are ideas that are at first seen as "radical" and then slowly accepted and assimilated. I believe it will help adults know where to look for proposed answers to certain philosophical questions or problems. Often it lends solace to people in crisis to learn that other people have been wrestling with these questions since human consciousness came online.

It should be noted that most of the below mentioned philosophers wrote thousands and thousands of pages (by hand, and on paper or papyrus in most cases) and that following them there are bookcases and bookcases of books commenting on all of their writings; thus, any attempt to reduce a philosopher's contribution to "The Conversation" that has been taking place over the past 2500 years is ludicrous. And yet, familiarizing yourself with the names of certain pivotal philosophers - those whose ideas shifted the paradigm or provided a gateway onto another avenue - might inspire you to re-envision adulthood from a fresh perspective.

In terms of glossing over interesting proposals from philosophers that may help contemporary adults reframe their current situations and perceptions, here is the most cursory list possible:

Plato (circa 427 BCE - 338 BCE). Leaving college students should be familiar with Plato's Allegory of the Cave, which essentially displays that we cannot rely on what we perceive through our senses to be "the truth" or even "reality." Everything that we perceive could just be an illusion. This will remain a constant theme in Western philosophy as philosophers discuss various "Matrix"-like possibilities.

Aristotle's (circa 384 BCE to 322 BCE) works covered all aspects of philosophy but for our purposes, as I discussed in "How To Survive Your Childhood Now That You're An Adult," he is important for our purposes because he asked the question, "What is the good life?" For us that will translate as "What are your measures of success and how did they arrive there?" Again, you were "thrown" into a culture and are probably familiar with concepts such as "The American Dream" and "The 40-hour work week." You did not create these ideas. Who is the author of your measure of "The Good Life."

Descartes (1596-1650) is famous for doubting everything except the fact that he could doubt. Thus he came up with his famous "Cogito Ergo Sum," which translates into "I think, therefore I am," and pivoted our entire civilization onto a misguided trajectory, in my humble opinion. These three words placed a primacy on thinking, on supposedly "rational" thought. Auschwitz was rational to the Nazis. Hiroshima was rational to the Americans. Fracking is rational to energy companies. Testing

164

pharmaceuticals on animals is rational. Razing the rainforest is rational. There are infinite examples of rationality ending dele- teriously. Sir Ken Robinson in his Ted Talk states that "In Amer- ica we primarily think of our bodies as transportation mecha- nisms for our heads." When Tibetans think of the word "mind" they point to their heart, not their head. I believe that Descartes' radical skepticism inevitably caused "Science" to throw the baby out with the bathwater and that 340 years later the "New Age" movement is an attempt to reconcile science with spirituality (which may not be possible).

Immanuel Kant (1724-1804) was an interesting fellow who is most widely known for his "Critique of Pure Reason," which is almost impossible to read. However, the proposition that would be helpful for collegians to take away from it is that there is an objective reality "out there" but we as individuals as we intuit through our senses can never be certain about it. For me, the most interesting thing Kant wrote about was categories of con- sciousness. The basic ways that humans perceive what is out there are through time and space. Our minds formulate things in terms of past, present, and future and try to ascribe causality, which is the main goal of our system of Science; and our five senses perceive space in terms of distance, colors, height, etc.

Like Kant, Georg Ludwig Hegel (1770-1831) wrote thou- sands of pages on all aspects of philosophy but what is important to take away from his rather obtuse "The Phenomenology of Spirit" is what we could know in relationship to what was tran- scendental "out there" - things that exist ubiquitously in humans a priori. The shift that we should observe starting with Hegel is his concentration on the study of consciousness and the objects

165

of direct experience. Kant's analysis is based on individual perception, but incorporates scientific understanding, logic and morality as well. Hegel's vision is much more grandiose, leading to an attempt at explaining virtually all human endeavors and how the world works, beginning with consciousness. For our purposes, one tenet that we should take away from Hegel is the falsely attributed concept of "dialectic," which I don't believe Hegel mentioned - but Fichte did mention it. It's essentially a formula for evolution that most notably Karl Marx used: Thesis plus Antithesis equals Synthesis. I would argue that the notion of dialectic is a huge problem; it's actually a foible of human consciousness that is built to think in antinomies - black/white, tall/short, small/large - and that this is the root cause of many of our society's major problems. Our minds perceive situations as "either/or" when they could also be seen as "both/and."

Nietzsche (1844-1900). For me, Nietzsche said everything. It's difficult to know where to start to introduce Nietzsche to someone who doesn't know his work, but for the purposes of this book regarding why Western adults become disillusioned, disenchanted and disappointed, I think it's best to begin here with his aphorism on "The Greatest Danger" and the conclusion of this book will advocate what Nietzsche wrote in his aphorism "One Thing is Needful."

Here's the first part of "The Greatest Danger":

The Greatest Danger. Had there not at all times been a larger number of men who regarded the cultivation of their mind - their "rationality" - as their pride, their obligation, their virtue, and were injured or shamed by all play of fancy

166

and extravagance of thinking - as lovers of "sound common sense" - mankind would long ago have perished! Incipient insanity has hovered, and hovers continually over mankind as its greatest danger: it is precisely the breaking out of inclination in feeling, seeing, and hearing; the enjoyment of the unruliness of the mind; the delight in human unreason. It is not truth and certainty that is the antithesis of the world of the insane, but the universality and all-obligatoriness of a belief, in short, non-voluntariness in forming opinions. And the greatest labour of human beings hitherto has been to agree with one another regarding a number of things, and to impose upon themselves a law of agreement - indifferent whether these things are true or false.

My understanding of this aphorism stated as briefly as possible is that for over eighteen hundred years members of Western civilization submitted themselves to an agreed array of laws that primarily were distilled from the Judeo-Christian bibles. For Nietzsche, the idea of god is malarkey, a complete and utter fiction; however, the fact that the majority of Westerners AGREED (albeit tacitly or subconsciously) to believe to some degree in this fiction precluded anarchy.

Calling the notion of god a fantasy as Nietzsche did in 1882 when he wrote "God is dead" constitutes an event, a rupture in our paradigm. Previously, in my humble estimation, even the greatest philosophers believed to some degree in a Christian ideal of god and just played semantic games by naming it things such as "Absolute Spirit." But Nietzsche, by his own acclaim, wrote with a hammer and I believe knew that his proclamation was as profound as declaring the earth was round after aeons of believing it was flat.

Nietzsche wrote thousands of pages of luscious and poetic and beautiful mind-twisting thoughts so it is a profound injustice to pull a few sentences and offer them to you as representing Nietzsche. However, for our purposes - to inspire you to revitalize your life and create actionable solutions to your disillusionment, disenchantment and disappointment - you need to know that it was Nietzsche who destroyed the illusion of the Christian god and created the possibility of Madonna - as well as YOU - constructing your life as if you were constructing a magnificent piece of art.

Martin Heidegger (1889 -1976) is controversial because of his affiliation with the Nazi party but for our purposes we need to be aware of his concept of "Being unto death." Humans are the only animals (to the best of our knowledge) who know they are going to die. I believe it is a "rite of passage" when a young person first sees another dead human and realizes that they also will someday die. Many times it results in what I refer to as teenage solipsism and even sometimes in hedonism. "What does anything matter?" teenagers are wont to ask. If we're all just going to die why do I need to study, work or do anything that doesn't bring me immediate gratification???" So I hope you see why human consciousness - as opposed to animal consciousness is both a blessing and a curse.

Jean-Paul Sartre (1905-1980): Sartre believed in the essential freedom of individuals, and he also believed that such freedom necessitated a responsibility for our own ways of seeing the world and our actions. On the other hand, besides his philosophical magnum opus "Being and Nothingness," Sartre wrote many plays and books. You are probably already familiar with his phrase from his play "No Exit," "L'enfer, c'est les autres," which is usually translated into English as "Hell is other people."

Ludwig Wittgenstein (1889–1951): Firstly, Wittgenstein is not usually considered a Continental philosopher because England, where he taught, is not a part of the continent and also Wittgenstein was more interested in Analytic Philosophy than the existentialism of despairing French and German thinkers. I have a different understanding of Wittgenstein than anyone I have ever met. I believe that the most important thing we can take away from Wittgenstein is his pedagogical method. The French word is "leurre" which is like "lure" the way bait lures a fish to bite a hidden hook. Another way of thinking about it is as teasing. If I say the world is flat, most of you will immediately say, "No, it isn't." But if I lure or tease towards entertaining a new possibility by asking a series of questions such as, "Look at the horizon - what do you see?" eventually I may lure you into other possibilities. We all have fairly fixed (and often wrong or misguided) understandings, perspectives and beliefs in our minds. And by "wrong" I mean that someday more accurate understandings, perspectives and beliefs will exist. Our understandings are ephemeral. And yet they seem concrete. So concrete that some fundamentalists are willing to kill and die for them. Thus, studying philosophy in university and "luring" students into thinking critically - entertaining a wide array of possibilities and then deciding which resonates most with them - is the beauty I saw in the way Wittgenstein formulated his questions and propositions.

Michel Foucault (1926-1984) studied "systems of thought." In particular, following Nietzsche, he thought that power was the central proponent behind much of human action and that the ability to control not only situations but other people led to such things as mental asylums and prisons. One can see that his arguments remain alive and well in Shoshana Zuboff's "The Age of Surveillance Capitalism: The Fight for a Human Future at the New Frontier of Power." Foucault first studied and taught "archeologies" that examined tranches or slices of history and then moved on to study and teach genealogies that studied transmutations or evolutions within cultures.

Jacques Derrida (1930-2004) Derrida argues that there are no self-sufficient units of meaning in a text, because individual words or sentences in a text can only be properly understood in terms of how they fit into the larger structure of the text and language itself. One famous quote is "There is nothing outside of (the) text" to which I would add that all "text" can be deconstructed - that the meaning can fall out from underneath the text or that there is no or not one "essential meaning." Everything is relative. Derrida is very controversial because much of his extensive oeuvre seems too playful to be philosophy. Derrida was an extremely interesting person and I recommend watching the documentary about him to try to gain some insights into the rupture for which he was responsible known as deconstruction.

Sociology

After psychology and philosophy it would be great for students to take one sociology course. And it would be even better if that course was taught by a radical leftist, a progressive, an idealist, someone wearing a beret. Sociology is the study of social life, social change, and the social causes and consequences of human behavior. Sociologists investigate the structure of groups, organizations, and societies and how people interact within these contexts. Since all human behavior is social, the subject matter of sociology ranges from the intimate family to the hostile mob; from organized crime to religious traditions; from the divisions of race, gender and social class to the shared beliefs of a common culture.

Since sociology primarily studies how humans interact, and they primarily interact in groups, besides all of the recent developments in gender studies and identity politics, I think it would benefit adults to understand that human beings are TRIBAL. We are preternaturally designed to live in tribes of about 140-150 people. The nuclear family - mother, father, son, daughter - is an aberration. It really does take a village. And if you were raised by a single parent or were a latch-key kid moving from household to household and gaining and losing stepsiblings every few years, it doesn't necessarily mean that you're going to join the Crips or the Bloods, but you may spend an undue amount of time subconsciously trying to find your "people." This may lead you down some dark alleys.

Even when people meet at a bar and ask, "What's your name? Where are you from? What do you do?" Or when people look at each other's name-brand handbags or automobiles or casually mention where they like to vacation. In marketing it's called "affinity grouping." The people in first class airport lounges feel more confident that members of their tribe are in first class

171

lounges. Golf clubs, tennis clubs, baseball teams, music fans, sports teams' fans… everyone is preternaturally looking for their tribe, people they can trust.

In olden days, people depended on their tribe to survive. If you betrayed your tribe by stealing or cheating they would eject you. And if you were ejected by one tribe the possibility was fairly high that no other tribe would accept you. Actually they probably would kill you. So the price for betrayal was extremely high. But late capitalism is so competitive and the stakes are so high that it is impossible to trust anyone. In "Super Capitalism" former treasury secretary Robert Reich claims that most American businesspeople do NOT take the two weeks vacation allotted to them per year because they fear an underling sabotaging them and replacing them while they are away. Yes, there are supposed leadership workshops and team-building weekends but in general we live in a "winner-takes-all" atmosphere of a highly competitive nature and given the opportunity to advance at the expense of others, usually people are quite selfish.

So taking one sociology class to learn how Karl Marx prophesied the decline of capitalism due to the increase disparity in classes and the subsequent growing resentment and animosity is important in case the 47% of Americans (today) are correct and there will be another American civil war in the near future.

Lastly, and this sociological comment relates to the next section on economics, students should leave university knowing Herbert Spencer's dictum (falsely attributed to Darwin) of "survival of the fittest." In the mid 19th century there was scarcity of resources so survival seemed like a zero-sum game, meaning that if you had a slice of the pie there was one less slice for me. But all of the inventions beginning with mass production during the industrial revolution now means that the planet does not have finite resources to support human life. However, that same mass production - razing rain forests, fish farming, meat production, fracking, big agriculture, mining precious metals, building huge factories, etc. - is now affecting climate change and making parts of the earth uninhabitable. Thus, studying sociology and learning how societies operate under systems such as capitalism and socialism is essential to know so that you can compare yourself with people in other societal situations.

Economics

Economics: in general, in my not so humble opinion, there's probably no subject more useless to study. There are some brilliant economists to study, such as Thomas Piketty and Robert Reich, but studying economic graphs and charts is inane. And here's why: think of Heisenberg's Uncertainty Principle: we can only measure the velocity OR the position of a particle at one time. So the "science" of economics is ludicrous because economists are holding infinite variables constant in order to measure a few isolated numbers. This has very little correlation to real life where those infinite variables are dynamic, constantly moving. So yes, in general, all other factors remaining constant, being able to say, "If we lower interest rates, then housing sales will rise," is accurate. However, "all other factors remaining constant" - especially when "all" is infinite and unpredictable - is one click left of useless. And if you analyze specific numbers and supposed indicators, such as "Gross Domestic Product" for instance, you will find that they are extremely poor indicators of overall quality of life or happiness. Orwell predicted and depicted all of what is occurring now very accurately: a large swath of society devotes inordinate mental space to watching arbitrary numbers on a screen go up and down. Understanding the backstory to these numbers will help people later in life stave off the depression and anxiety that reasonably ensues when your emotional life is hitched to a financial rollercoaster. Thus, having a general understanding of concepts such as inflation, the Federal Reserves, bonds, and myriad indices will help you "bet" your earnings on more historically profitable financial institutions and vehicles. However, it may also teach you to expect the unexpected and not to rely heavily on Jim Cramer or any economists who claim to be smarter than lucky with their predictions.

History

Knowledge of the history of our culture is necessary if we want to avoid making the same mistakes over and over. Historians have a great sense of the direction that our society is headed because they can pinpoint the ruptures and events that spun the way people behaved over time. Knowing about the causes of war, how different governments evolved, and the history of tectonic shifting inventions such as banking, urban planning, photography, audio recording, the first computer, radio waves, air travel, medical advance, etc. will help you gain a greater appreciation for the privileges and luxuries that we all enjoy. Many of us cannot imagine life without our mobile phones but imagine the expression of joy your great grandparents had when their outhouse was replaced by an indoor toilet. What about the history of bridges linking various plots of land? All of the things we accept as "normal" are relatively recent inventions. 400 years ago, I would be writing this book by dipping a quill into an ink jar; 150 years ago I would be writing this book with a fountain pen; 100 years ago I might be typing it on a typewriter (as I typed all of my papers in college); and for the last 30 years nearly everything we write is some form of ones and zeros that miraculously appear on a glass screen. I can now even speak most of this book into a microphone and it will be dictated as typed text. Even if you're not the beneficiary of an organ transplant or some life-saving surgery or medicine, knowing that your quality of life is infinitely higher in many ways than previous generations will help you surmount the crises we now experience in adulthood.

It is important to study history to understand that all of the mores and customs that you and I consider to be "normal" in one-hundred years will surely seem absurd. Everything that we consider "normal" in our daily life today will be considered the way we consider the feudal system sooner than we think.

English/English Literature

Language creates reality. If you cannot articulate your thoughts as precisely (and compassionately) as possible then you are operating at an extreme deficit. Knowing how to speak and write as concisely and accurately as possible is essential to engendering compassionate relationships, the one thing that correlates strongly with overall happiness. Thus, studying English as is done at university primarily by studying literature, is one of the most important skills to learn while at school.

Similarly, knowledge of the history of English literature will help understand all other academic disciplines. When young people ask me what they should study if they want to learn psychology, I always reply, "Shakespeare." All human emotions and dynamics after the bibles were pivoted into modern thought by William Shakespeare. Shakespeare wrestled with all aspects of human nature and American and British writers since him make use of conventions that he invented. Although I found and still find Shakespeare arduous to read, when one sees the plays and then reads the words it becomes apparent how much of our tropes were created by him.

After Shakespeare it is important to be aware of the different epochs of literature in Western civilization such as exploration, colonialism, realism, romanticism, revolution, modernity, postmodernity and contemporary literature will improve all of your relationships. Again, as in painting and music, each epoch correlates to a rupture in general consciousness that eventually leads to a pivot. The first performances of Stravinsky's "Rite of Spring" in Paris caused rioting; today it's a regular part of the LA Philharmonic's repertoire. Joyce's books were banned; now you can study them at most universities. Being able to trace contemporary crises and ruptures as they have appeared in literature through the past 500 years will allow you to have enlightening intellectual conversations and people will want to interact with you more if you can engage in intelligent conversations about the common themes that have threaded our society's literary and artistic canons.

Art History

Like literature, the epochs of art and the ruptures that spun certain movements into new directions will help improve all of your relationships. For aeons paintings and sculptures were created to tell stories, from cave paintings all the way through the renaissance. And then there was art for the sake of art, to create beauty, to explore romanticism, to concretize ephemeral sensuality, to investigate consciousness.

Personally - and this relates to Chapter 3 regarding dating and intimate relationships - I think you learn more about another human being by strolling through a museum together than by interviewing them at Starbucks. Knowing which epochs appeal to you and why will tell more about your personality than the Meyers-Briggs exam. Do you know why millions of people flock to the Louvre to stand in front of the Mona Lisa for a few minutes? Can you identify the unique subtle soft yellow light coming through the window in most of Vermeer's paintings? Can you tell the different intentions of romantic vs. realist painters? Do impressionistic paintings fill you with a joyous calm? Can you re-create in your mind a guitar that a cubist painter deconstructed? Does your mind try to form patterns and shapes when you stand in front of a Jackson Pollock, Barnett Newman or Ellsworth Kelly? What do you feel that Rothko's paintings are pointing towards or indicating? Or maybe Magritte and Duchamp and the absurdity indicated by surrealists makes your heart chuckle?

As already mentioned, art, literature, poetry, photography, film, and music are all part of what I call "The Conversation." They provide commonalities for you and me to discuss. Different artworks resonate or don't resonate with us at different times in our lives. Being able to trace through the epochs of art and know which ones are beautiful and meaningful to you will help you transcend the crises that artists have been investigating since art began to exist for art's sake.

Film/Film Theory

Film, film theory: the *sturm und drang* of the human experience has been documented and fictionalized by filmmakers for the past hundred years. Although the genre of "documentary" has mostly devolved into propaganda, it is worthwhile to watch those few exquisite docs where the filmmakers themselves are surprised and end up taking the audience on a completely unimagined journey. Regarding narrative films, in America films are mostly viewed for the purpose of entertainment. However, like literature, music, painting, and other art forms, films are able to convey extremely precise emotions that many of us will eventually encounter. In the old days, when people went to movie theaters and sat silently in the dark without phones vibrating in their pockets, there was a tacit contract made between the filmmaker and the spectator; in particular, the French "New Wave" and other genre-bending, rule-breaking films allow audience members to enter other realities, other cultures, other times. The magic of film is the way genius directors have altered time to create non-linear narratives that grab the audience members and shake up their paradigms. Taking a class on film theory and history will open students' eyes up to new realities that they otherwise may never experience.

Music

Having a passionate and articulate fellow human explain the motifs and intricacies of classical music, jazz and then contemporary music is priceless. And learning about music - like painting - would expose newly minted adults to the spiritual quests that composers such as Gustav Mahler and John Coltrane were on.

World Religions/Spirituality

My personal opinion is that the negatives - crusades, wars, pedophilia, hypocrisy, financial greed - of all organized religions outweigh the positives and that planet earth will be better off when all religions are in the dustbin of history. However, it is possible for people to be spiritual and for there to be positive, supportive spiritual communities and rituals without having the negatives that have pervaded organized religions.

And as an aside, please note that Buddhism should not be considered a religion; it is a humanistic psychology designed to alleviate the suffering caused by human consciousness. Anyone who considers Buddhism a religion can go to hell (ha ha).

Anyhow, as I mentioned regarding Carl Jung above (but really Schopenhauer), exposure to world (non-Western) cultures, beliefs systems and paradigms will greatly lend immediate solace if not solutions to later adult crises. Knowing that other cultures have 5,000 year-old practices for treating sundry afflictions and ailments would at least complement our scientific, Western medical model.

179

Briefly, witnessing the interest in yoga in America, it is beneficial to pursue an extremely brief overview of Hinduism: for thousands of years all over the world humans have been trying to commune with the divine. Yoga means union. During the Vedic period c. 1500 – c. 500 BCE yoga was a group of men shouting around a fire in order to connect with God, various gods, and/or Brahman. The end of the Vedic period culminated in the Upanishads which ended up being thousands of written vignettes pointing towards the divine. For example, "Tat tvam asi" or "Thou art that." Essentially, to reduce the thousands of pages of Upanishads to a fortune cookie, I would write "Atman equals Brahman." The individual soul is actually at one, united, with everythingness/god/the divine/Brahman and everything that we perceive through our five senses and chunk into a narrative is "maya" or superficial and ephemeral. Leaving college with a brief overview of Hinduism and a few experiences with yoga and meditation may loosen a younger adult's clenched grip on their faith in science. For example, over the years I have treated clients who had experienced "Kundalini Rising experiences" which can be extremely frightening. Thus, some knowledge of the chakra system and kundalini energy as well as the koshas and doshas would be extremely profitable for those psychonauts who experiment with DMT, ayahuasca, psilocybin, LSD, Ketamine, MDMA or any of the designer drugs that are coming out. Similarly, via Hinduism, disillusioned couples can find their way through yoga to studying and practicing tantra and tantric sex, which may also help alleviate some mid-life crises.

The Buddha (c. 6th to 5th century BCE or c. 5th to 4th century BCE) was a Hindu the way Jesus was a Jew. He was a prince whose father sequestered him because he didn't want him to see pain, suffering and death. When Buddha finally left the castle he saw pain, suffering and death and then went on a long journey to uncover the origins of pain, suffering, and death. And while he did not overcome death, he developed quite a comprehensive protocol to alleviate suffering - particularly the type of suffering you are probably experiencing if you picked up a book entitled "Wired & Tired." Buddhism is a humanistic psychology, not a religion. It has provided solace for billions of practitioners for thousands of years.

Other

Lastly, all universities should have some sort of "How To Adult" or "How To Be An Adult" or "How To Behave Like An Adult" or "How To Act Like An Adult" mandatory course before shuffling that year's lemmings into the capitalist abyss. Here are some of the subjects that should be covered in such a curriculum:

- How to lead a balanced life
- How to be responsible
- What to expect from marriage
- What to expect from your first job(s)
- How to pay bills on time
- How to make your life meaningful
- How to speak to authority figures such as the police
- How to create community
- How to keep your sense of wonder and curiosity alive: Beginner's Mind
- Skills for maintaining compassionate relationships
- Giving back, being of service, teaching, making the world a better place

181

- How you became you
- Radical generosity and compassion
- How to breathe, meditate, self-regulate
- How to be grateful
- How to have a healthy relationship with money
- How to stay physically healthy
- How to eat to fuel your body and not for psychological reasons
- How to have healthy relationships with drugs and alcohol

In addition, I wouldn't be opposed to classes such as "What is Affection?" "What is Non-Verbal Communication?" "What are the best ways to keep up with world events?" "How to give a non-creepy hug," "How to avoid getting raped," "How to have non-dysfunctional relationships that are still fun," etc.

Lastly (yes, you should always save the best for last), sex education should not only be taught in middle school and high school, but upon leaving university all students should have to pass an exam showing that they have sufficient knowledge of how human beings both procreate and recreate. Procreational sex is when you have the intention of producing a baby and recreational sex is when you have the explicit intention of NOT producing a baby.

In his book "Constructing the Sexual Crucible: An Integration of Sexual and Marital Therapy," David Schnarch posits that sexual intercourse in America has become akin to mutual masturbation, that the way we approach recreational sex is too goal oriented, too focused on orgasm; thus, for some couples intercourse has become more like a business transaction than a mindful, loving, connective, passionate, intimate experience. Esther

Perel in her TED talk opines that passionate, intimate sex and marriage may unwittingly be mutually exclusive because "How can you desire what you already have?"

So what then is the purpose of recreational sex, when people are expressly trying to avoid making a baby?

If aliens from another galaxy wanted to know how human beings procreate they would not have a problem. Procreative sex is primal, intuitive. However, if aliens typed "sex" into Google I think that they would be bemused by the sexual activities our species engages in when we are not procreating. The first question the aliens might pose is, "Recreational sex seems to have become very athletic. Do some people consider it to be a form of calisthenics, a.k.a. 'sexercise'"?

Next they might query, "Why are so many humans spritzing each other with bodily fluids? Is this an expression of love? Or are they like dogs urinating on trees to mark their territories?" Then the aliens would probably be befuddled by the multifarious usage of rectums, which - if I am not mistaken - were primarily designed as one-way streets and now, according to the Internet, are being employed as twelve lane freeways. Then I believe that they would find the use of masturbation as a sleep-aid, a meditation, a warm-up act, or a "release" from the daily stresses, disappointments and traumas of highly competitive capitalism to be somewhat bizarre, imprudent, and alarming. Lastly, I believe, the aliens would ponder if there are any concrete relationships between sex, intimacy and love? And what are the ideal circumstances and conditions that create lasting passion? Let us assume that one of these aliens took a human form and we wanted to explain to him or her nonprocreational sex as a mindful, loving, connective, passionate, intimate experience. What would we say?

We might say that there are infinite ways of having sex, infinite ways of showing love, and infinite ways of being intimate with another human being. However, the lexicon is rather dynamic so when two people (or three or four or five) want to be intimate, the best way to avoid problems is to have an open and honest conversation about the way each individual likes to explore, the pace each individual feels comfortable with, the boundaries each individual has, and some of the things in the past that the individual has found pleasing and displeasing. AND THEN THEY NEED TO FORGET THAT THIS CONVERSATION EVER TOOK PLACE! Because giving someone an instruction manual or road map to your body destroys the moment, destroys authenticity, destroys presence, destroys intimacy, destroys passion.

Recognize that your mind projects your own bodily pleasures onto your partners' bodies and this is completely misguided. Just because you enjoy having your neck kissed in a certain way or your arm stroked in a certain manner doesn't mean that anyone else does. Any assumptions regarding what pleases or displeases another human being are fallacious and the only way to bridge this chasm is through authentic communications and loving explorations. Also recognize that your body and what pleases it will change over time and your partner's body and what pleases it will change over time. This could be referred to as personal "sexual evolution" and it is a good thing seeing as we are primed to crave novelty; as a species we get bored rather easily. Thus, activities that you once considered illicit or verboten will become more and more titillating as you evolve (mostly due to the fact that you considered them illicit or verboten) and you may eventually become drawn to them like a moth to a flame.

In summary, if younger adults have primarily learned about sex from pornography and want to now have intimate adult encounters, then it would be beneficial for them to take classes where they learn that:

1. All interactions must be 100% consensual
2. There is no inherent relationship between sex, intimacy, and love and that any assumptions you make will probably end up ruining whatever connection you are trying to create
3. They should be invested in having an open conversation about what their partner considers to be loving and pleasurable signs of affection
4. Forget everything they have ever learned about sex as teenagers and particularly anything they have ever seen on the Internet
5. Be committed to showing up authentically and discussing any traumas and shame
6. Create the physical space so that you can be physically naked without distractions (such as nosy neighbors or police officers)
7. Create the mental space so that you can be mentally naked and present (and release fears from the past and expectations about the imminent future)
8. Create the emotional space to be emotionally naked (and vulnerable)

9. For non-atheists, create the spiritual space to be spiritually open to connecting with and being intimate with a fellow human being (and having whatever is divine in you touch whatever is divine in them)

10. Disregard any techniques or anything you ever learned from any other human body including your own

11. Have a sense of wonder and explore with unbiased curiosity. Or more precisely, be as present as humanly possible and do your utmost to attune to how your partner is breathing and moving and feeling at that very moment. If you catch your mind wandering forwards or backwards or sideways gently guide it back into focusing on the sensations on your hands, lips and other sensitive body parts

I'm fairly certain that I'm not going to be the president of a university anytime soon; however, I hope that I have made it obvious to all that 1. being intellectually curious and 2. having refined "soft skills" will help preclude becoming wired & tired and if you are already wired & tired then studying any or all of the above will help you revitalize your life.

The goal of university should be to widen students' horizons and provide them with more choices and opportunities. Life is analogous to a tree and the more you know and experience, than the more the tree will bloom, blossom and prosper. College should be a time of unbridled and unfettered wonder and curiosity and I hope that my brief gloss-over some of my favorite disciplines - psychology, philosophy, sociology, history, music, art history, literature and world religions (spirituality) - would help prepare people for a more even keel, a less dramatic adulthood.

The world would be a much more peaceful place if each newly minted adult understood that every person has their own individual epistemological paradigm that constitutes what they consider to be "normal." According to much of Western psychology, these paradigms exist in our unconscious minds. Phenomena outside of these paradigms are often viewed as strange, frightening or absurd when they impinge on our conscious minds. However, I believe that a wide breadth of liberal arts education is able to make us see outside of our "normals" in ways that are not found to be excessively strange, terribly frightening or patently absurd. Instead of spending our lives trying to dogmatically inflict our personal perspectives on other people, understanding that there are different ways of perceiving reality might allow us to live together more compassionately.

Conclusions

Most people I meet feel wired & tired: over-worked, over-stimulated, under-loved, and under-appreciated. There's an odd malaise hovering over our society due to the constant fears and stresses that we consider to be "normal." We have lost what is essential to the human experience and instead frantically fritter away our days in front of sundry glass screens. We need to revitalize our lives.

Chapter 1 of this book provided a list of daily practices that you should incorporate to help revitalize your life. And as I discussed in Chapter 8, I propose a five-fold path to authenticity which I believe is relatively simple to understand and follow, namely Attachment, Atonement, Attunement, Presence and Congruence. After showing up authentically for our relationships, we can tweak our own operating systems from devolving into teenage nihilism - "What's the point? We're all going to die anyhow!" - by consciously deciding to live "**awakened**" lives. For me, being awakened means to embrace "and" rather than "either/or." The dialectical nature of the mind, finding antinomies such as tall/short, white/black, far/close, love/hate is the essential problem of many of both our planetary and individual problems. The dialectic is a foible of human consciousness. This is why it is important to have studied philosophy in college: because learning that 300 years ago Kant proposed that there is an objective reality "out there" but that humans could only have their individual subjective experiences and understandings of it makes a strong case for RELATIVISM. Relativism means that all truth claims are culturally contingent and that we need to accept that each individual person's reality - their notion of the color red, their notion of morality, their notion of propriety - is going to be different. The opposite of relativism is DOGMATISM, which means that people (fundamentally) - fundamentalists - believe that their views are the only "correct" and accurate views and thus must be inflicted on all other people for the benefit of everyone. Dogmatists try to reify their own beliefs by inflicting these beliefs on others, hence the Crusades, hence the Jihadists, hence the Nazis and white supremacists. People do not need to kill other people who do not share their understandings of reality; these immature power grabs have caused countless murders throughout history. In a society of relativists, everyone would ACCEPT the right of people to disagree with them and this would not cause fighting. Instead, our society is moving in the opposite direction thanks to both legacy media - Fox News vs CNN - and social media. "Echo chambers" have been created where people only receive news with which they already agree. These echo chambers create parallel realities and more and more intolerance, non-acceptance, which is why it currently appears that humans are too ignorant to create systemic change until AFTER a tremendous tragedy such as a war.

But it starts on the individual level. It starts with YOU. It starts with you being congruent and having personal integrity and using tools that will help you create a paradigmatic life that inspires others to show up as their highest selves. I believe that my path to leading an awakened life is synonymous with you showing up as your highest self.

Try this supposed dialectic on for size: life is inherently absurd and meaningless AND my mind craves coherence and meaning. I need meaning to get out of bed in the morning. For me, being awakened means not allowing teenage nihilism to overwhelm you. To embrace your passions and **create** a meaningful life full of loving relationships. Awakening is my combination of existential philosophy, narrative psychotherapy, and Buddhism - all of which were already discussed and all of which I believe you should have been studied in our educational system.

Again, the basic problem is that the mind and possibly the human brain or prefrontal cortex is primarily an either/or machine. If you really think about it, most of our concepts only exist in relation to their opposites: black/white, tall/short, rich/poor, love/hate, etc. F. Scott Fitzgerald wrote, "The test of a first-rate intelligence is the ability to hold two opposed ideas in mind at the same time and still retain the ability to function." When I teach I use optical illusions such as the rabbit/duck image to show students that they cannot hold opposed thoughts in their minds at the same time. Again, I believe that this is a foible of human consciousness and that philosophers of mind should examine this quality more rigorously. It's a serious problem, in my humble opinion. Awakening is learning to surf the paradoxes or apparent aporias of life and consciousness. And this is also why I advocate and teach meditation: meditation is an analogy for how we should lead our lives because it asks us to be alert and relaxed at the same time, a paradox. For now I am asking you to entertain the possibility that awakening is understanding how your mind inherently works (as a binary machine), how it was programmed (unintentionally) by how it chose to react to childhood traumas that occurred during the different individuation processes, knowing why you think what you think and how you became who you are, THEN making lifestyle choices or at least tweaks so that you can be the person you know you should be and live the life that you know you should be living.

For me, after learning about spirituality I was able to tweak the narrative of my life to accept why I became who I am. After 25 years of having an adverse relationship with the scars on my face, I consciously chose what was hitherto unfathomable. "I'm supposed to have these scars on my face. I'm supposed to have permanent discomfort," I uttered. Since I'll never be able to go back in time and remove my scars, the sooner that I stopped wanting to change the unchangeable, the sooner I would be able to alleviate the woulda-shoulda-coulda-didn't resentments that used to keep me awake at night. Narrative therapists help clients choose more propitious illusions. And this is what I consider to be leading an "awakened" life - to know that you are choosing the most accurate and propitious illusion possible, the one that will help engender authentic and compassionate relationships and keep you at the high end of your happiness spectrum. Atonement is tantamount to OWNING all of your history and threading it with a narrative so that you understand your triggers and compensations and why you became who you are today. Once you OWN your life you will stop the resentment-making machine - woulda-coulda-shoulda-didn't - that is actually at the root of much of your disillusionment, disenchantment and disappointment.

The crisis or rupture that led you to this book temporarily crushed your faith in the reality into which you were thrown and may not have previously questioned. The systems of education, healthcare, labor, capitalism, democracy, working 40 hours in 5 days per week, fossil fuels, pharmaceuticals, vacations, status symbols - all of the things that most people consider to be "normal" - are now seen as contingent, contingent on language, on society, on infinite factors. But now you know that this "normal" does not bring with it happiness. Actually, it is this "normal" that causes people to be wired & tired, anxious and depressed. So you are reading this book because you want to minimize anxiety and depression, you are sick of feeling wired & tired, and you want to construct a life that will be more favorable for keeping you at the higher range of your happiness spectrum. From the Harvard longitudinal study we know that the primary thing that correlates with happiness is the quality of our intimate relationships. From the studies on Attachment Theory, we all know that most of us have fairly unrefined tools to being in intimate relationships. My proposal is that our best shot for being in secure relationships is to learn how to be authentic. To make conscious choices and to have the personal integrity to abide by those choices. To be congruent. To know why we think the shit that we think (and by 'shit' I mean our fears and prejudices, the paradigms we developed from our insecure attachment dynamics) and to lean into being vulnerable and authentic.

This summarizes my 35 years of studying happiness through the disciplines of psychology, philosophy, spirituality and sociology, and what it would behoove people to study in order to lead balanced lives and have resources to stave off potential existential crises. I do not believe that I'm saying anything new in this book.

192

I have merely gleaned some nuggets from "The Conversation" of Western civilization to provide a fresh perspective that hopefully inspires you to revitalize your life.

As Nietzsche wrote:

"One thing is needful. -- To "give style" to one's character-- a great and rare art! It is practiced by those who survey all the strengths and weaknesses of their nature and then fit them into an artistic plan until every one of them appears as art and reason and even weaknesses delight the eye. Here a large mass of second nature has been added; there a piece of original nature has been removed -- both times through long practice and daily work at it. Here the ugly that could not be removed is concealed; there it has been reinterpreted and made sublime. Much that is vague and resisted shaping has been saved and exploited for distant views; it is meant to beckon toward the far and immeasurable. In the end, when the work is finished, it becomes evident how the constraint of a single taste governed and formed everything large and small. Whether this taste was good or bad is less important than one might suppose, if only it was a single taste! It will be the strong and domineering natures that enjoy their finest gaiety in such constraint and perfection under a law of their own; the passion of their tremendous will relaxes in the face of all stylized nature, of all conquered and serving nature. Even when they have to build palaces and design gardens, they demur at giving nature freedom. Conversely, it is the weak characters without power over themselves that hate the constraint of style. They feel that if this bitter and evil constraint were imposed upon them they would be demeaned; they become slaves as soon as they serve; they hate to serve.

Such spirits -- and they may be of the first rank -- are always out to shape and interpret their environment as free nature: wild, arbitrary, fantastic, disorderly, and surprising. And they are well advised because it is only in this way that they can give pleasure to themselves. For one thing is needful: that a human being should attain satisfaction with himself, whether it be by means of this or that poetry or art; only then is a human being at all tolerable to behold. Whoever is dissatisfied with himself is continually ready for revenge, and we others will be his victims, if only by having to endure his ugly sight. For the sight of what is ugly makes one bad and gloomy."

People in Western culture enjoy freedom and privileges than almost any other culture that has ever existed. And yet, there are twin epidemics of anxiety and depression plaguing our nation and contributing to our horrifying opioid addiction problem as well as our relatively high suicide rate. Few of us were given "User's Manuals" for our minds. My wish is that this book lends some comforting narratives regarding why we think what we think and how we can make healthier conscious decisions that will help us think in the most interesting, compassionate, loving, and joyous ways possible.

If there is any benefit to be gleaned from the recent pandemic(s), wars and natural disasters, it is that all of our systems have become corrupted, the old paradigms are moribund, and it is up to us to create a new way of interacting based on love instead of fear, on compassion rather than competition.

194

All of the things that we consider to be "normal" including going to university and working a 40-hour work week as well as "the nuclear family" should be questioned. All systems have been corrupted and we're amidst rampant erosion of the ground we have been standing on since the industrial revolution. It is time to create a new society, a society not based on survival of the fittest, scarcity-modeled zero-sum game, competition, and bottom lines. We need a new system that isn't based on oppression and exploitation. And the time to do so is today. Before the planet hemorrhages our little species of thinkers off of it with tsunamis, fires, tornadoes, hurricanes, plagues, diseases, undrinkable water and unbreathable air.

So instead of swiping your device to check your portfolio this morning, younger adults should ask what tremendous, life-enhancing, beautiful, compassionate, new idea or artwork or song or technology is waiting to enter the world through them? Nobody was put on earth to labor in order to make other rich people richer. All adults need to learn their callings as soon as possible and try to find jobs that facilitate the highest expression of their creative abilities. So long as we have enough money to subsist, any job that is only done for the sake of earning more money and doesn't fulfill our purpose, will end up making us feel wired & tired.

So you are either going to leave this book with new tools and practices, new solutions and results, or with excuses. Change is difficult - we fear change - and I hope that my passion for psychology, philosophy, spirituality and other subjects is infectious;

I hope that my passion inspires you to try new solutions to old problems.

To summarize, here is a resume of some of the tools and practices that I believe will bring you both immediate and long-term changes and results:

- The 3-part breath to take you out of fight or flight mode
- The problem-solving exercise to remember that we're often our own worst enemies
- Clap last Thursday: you can't change the past
- Metta Meditation - be the change you want to see in the world
- Clarity of consciousness, communication and sentiment
- Replace the resentments your mind creates with gratitude - write gratitude lists
- Reflective listening to help make others feel heard
- Being aware of your core wound of abandonment, betrayal
- Being aware of your mind's propensity for either/or
- Non-violent communications to express yourself authentically without blame
- Nadi Shodhana to balance your energies
- Forgiveness to clean up your resentments
- Accident Victims, Lottery Winners - things you think will make you happy will definitely make you happy but not for as long as you think they will
- Yoga to still the fluctuations of the mind
- Mindfulness meditations - learn to observe your thoughts rather than allowing them to drag you around
- Choosing relativism over dogmatism
- Congruence - deciding the life you want to lead and then figuring out how to create that life

And here are some of the excuses I've heard in my classes when people are too afraid to try new solutions:

- I didn't care for Ira
- I was overwhelmed by the material
- I've heard it all before
- I don't agree with Ira's politics
- This stuff is way too bohemian for me, too woo-woo for me
- Is "Ira Israel" a stage name?
- I have a migraine
- I think I missed some of the essential parts in the beginning
- Doesn't Ira know long hair is out of style?
- I'm too tired to read!
- I can't concentrate!
- (enter your usual excuse here)

I hope that this book has opened infinite new doors and shined a light on all of the ways that you can cultivate your sense of wonder, stop making excuses, add more tools to your psychological and emotional toolboxes, commit to scientifically proven daily practices to keep you at the high end of your happiness spectrum, revitalize your life, and stop feeling wired & tired.

Ira Israel
Santa Monica, California
November 17th, 2022

Acknowledgements

Eva Gardner was the first to read this book and contribute invaluable comments that improved the substance and presentation of the book immensely. Tara Dhillon and Ginevra Are Cappiello also provided wildly helpful suggestions and I'm grateful for the authentic compassion and love that Eva, Tara, and Ginevra have shown me. I'm also forever grateful to John Newell for helping me format the book and Jean Benedict Raffa for giving me notes.

Over the past 35 years I have had the immense fortune to interact with many first-rate thinkers who have inspired me including Reverend Michael Beckwith, Marianne Williamson, Jai Uttal, Rick Hanson, Paul Hawken, Esther Perel, Fred Luskin, James Baraz, Phillip Moffitt, David Richo, Jack Kornfield, Alan Wallace, David Gordon White, Barbara Holdrege, Alexander Nehamas, Philip Rieff and Samuel McCormick. For all of their support, patience, and tolerance over the past thirty years, I must thank Don Henry, Margaret Daniel, Stuart Cohen, Eric DelaBarre, Jennifer Markson, Theodore Kyriakos, Jeff Faski, Rachel Bargiel, Michelle Friedman, Josephine Wallace, Felicia Tomasko, Emmanuel Itier, Jerome Mercier, Irving Schwartz, Natalie and David Jones, Sting, Jack Kornfield, Shauna Shapiro, Warren Farrell, Katherine Woodward Thomas, Joanne Cacciatore, Linda Bloom, Larry Payne, Fred Luskin, Laetitia Arrighi, Joel Friedlander, Gary Klein, Matt Berman, Marielle Yehouetome, Jasmin Palmer, John Newell, Donna Goldman, Ruth and Steven Haworth, Anne Brochet, Chantal Moltini, Lauren Michael, and Dr. Edward Ines and his amazing staff.

About the Author

Ira Israel is a Licensed Professional Clinical Counselor and Licensed Marriage and Family Therapist. He graduated from the University of Pennsylvania and holds graduate degrees in psychology, philosophy, and religious studies. Ira is the author of "How To Survive Your Childhood Now That You're An Adult: A Path to Authenticity and Awakening" and the creator of the DVDs "A Beginner's Guide to Happiness," "A Beginner's Guide to Mindfulness Meditation," "Mindfulness Meditations for Anxiety," "Mindfulness for Urban Depression" and "Yoga for Depression and Anxiety."

For more information, please visit www.IraIsracl.com

Made in the USA
Middletown, DE
19 November 2022